JAMESTOWN EDUCATION

Timed Readings Plus in Mathematics

BOOK 1

15 Two-Part Lessons with Questions for Building Reading Fluency and Comprehension

McGraw Hill Glencoe

New York, New York   Columbus, Ohio   Chicago, Illinois   Peoria, Illinois   Woodland Hills, California

JAMESTOWN EDUCATION

Glencoe

The McGraw-Hill Companies

ISBN: 0-07-872659-X

Send all queries to:
Glencoe/McGraw-Hill
8787 Orion Place
Columbus, OH 43240-4027

3 4 5 6 7 8 9 10 ROV 15 14 13 12 11 10

CONTENTS

To the Student

You probably talk at an average rate of about 150 words a minute. If you are a reader of average ability, you read at a rate of about 250 words a minute. So your reading speed is nearly twice as fast as your speaking or listening speed. This example shows that reading is one of the fastest ways to get information.

The purpose of this book is to help you increase your reading rate and understand what you read. The 15 lessons in this book will also give you practice in reading mathematics-related articles and in preparing for tests in which you must read and understand nonfiction passages within a certain time limit.

Reading Faster and Better

Following are some strategies that you can use to read the articles in each lesson.

Previewing

Previewing before you read is a very important step. This helps you to get an idea of what a selection is about and to recall any previous knowledge you have about the subject. Here are the steps to follow when previewing.

Read the title. Titles are designed not only to announce the subject but also to make the reader think. Ask yourself questions such as What can I learn from the title? What thoughts does it bring to mind? What do I already know about this subject?

Read the first sentence. If it is short, read the first two sentences. The opening sentence is the writer's opportunity to get your attention. Some writers announce what they hope to tell you in the selection. Some writers state their purpose for writing; others just try to get your attention.

Read the last sentence. If it is short, read the final two sentences. The closing sentence is the writer's last chance to get ideas across to you. Some writers repeat the main idea once more. Some writers draw a conclusion—this is what they have been leading up to. Other writers summarize their thoughts; they tie all the facts together.

Skim the entire selection. Glance through the selection quickly to see what other information you can pick up. Look for anything that will help you read fluently and with understanding. Are there names, dates, or numbers? If so, you may have to read more slowly.

Reading for Meaning

Here are some ways to make sure you are making sense of what you read.

Build your concentration. You cannot understand what you read if you are not concentrating. When you discover that your thoughts are straying, correct the situation right away. Avoid distractions and distracting situations. Keep in mind the information you learned from previewing. This will help focus your attention on the selection.

Read in thought groups. Try to see meaningful combinations of words—phrases, clauses, or sentences. If you look at only one word at a time (called word-by-word reading), both your comprehension and your reading speed suffer.

Ask yourself questions. To sustain the pace you have set for yourself and to maintain a high level of concentration and comprehension, ask yourself questions such as What does this mean? or How can I use this information? as you read.

Finding the Main Ideas

The paragraph is the basic unit of meaning. If you can quickly discover and understand the main idea of each paragraph, you will build your comprehension of the selection.

Find the topic sentence. The topic sentence, which contains the main idea, often is the first sentence of a paragraph. It is followed by sentences that support, develop, or explain the main idea. Sometimes a topic sentence comes at the end of a paragraph. When it does, the supporting details come first, building the base for the topic sentence. Some paragraphs do not have a topic sentence; all of the sentences combine to create a meaningful idea.

Understand paragraph structure. Every well-written paragraph has a purpose. The purpose may be to inform, define, explain, or illustrate. The purpose should always relate to the main idea and expand on it. As you read each paragraph, see how the body of the paragraph tells you more about the main idea.

Relate ideas as you read. As you read the selection, notice how the writer puts together ideas. As you discover the relationship between the ideas, the main ideas come through quickly and clearly.

Mastering Reading Comprehension

Reading fast is not useful if you don't remember or understand what you read. The two exercises in Part A provide a check on how well you have understood the article.

Recalling Facts

These multiple-choice questions provide a quick check to see how well you recall important information from the article. As you learn to apply the reading strategies described earlier, you should be able to answer these questions more successfully.

Understanding Ideas

These questions require you to think about the main ideas in the article. Some main ideas are stated in the article; others are not. To answer some of the questions, you need to draw conclusions about what you read.

The five exercises in Part B require multiple answers. These exercises provide practice in applying comprehension and critical thinking skills that you can use in all your reading.

Recognizing Words in Context

Always check to see whether the words around an unfamiliar word—its context—can give you a clue to the word's meaning. A word generally appears in a context related to its meaning.

Suppose, for example, that you are unsure of the meaning of the word *expired* in the following passage:

> Vera wanted to check out a book, but her library card had expired. She had to borrow my card, because she didn't have time to renew hers.

You could begin to figure out the meaning of *expired* by asking yourself a question such as, What could have happened to Vera's library card that would make her need to borrow someone else's card? You might realize that if Vera had to renew her card, its usefulness must have come to an end or run out. This would lead you to conclude that the word *expired* must mean "to come to an end" or "to run out." You would be right. The context suggested the meaning.

Context can also affect the meaning of a word you already know. The word *key,* for instance, has many meanings. There are musical keys, door keys, and keys to solving a mystery. The context in which the word *key* occurs will tell you which meaning is correct.

Sometimes a word is explained by the words that immediately follow it. The subject of a sentence and your knowledge about that subject might also help you determine the meaning of an unknown word. Try to decide the meaning of the word *revive* in the following sentence:

> Sunshine and water will revive those drooping plants.

The compound subject is *sunshine* and *water.* You know that plants need light and water to survive and that drooping plants are not healthy. You can figure out that *revive* means "to bring back to health."

Distinguishing Fact from Opinion

Every day you are called upon to sort out fact and opinion. Because much of what you read and hear contains both facts and opinions, you need to be able to tell the two apart.

Facts are statements that can be proved. The proof must be objective and verifiable. You must be able to check for yourself to confirm a fact.

Look at the following facts. Notice that they can be checked for accuracy and confirmed. Suggested sources for verification appear in parentheses.

- Abraham Lincoln was the 16th president of the United States. (Consult biographies, social studies books, encyclopedias, and similar sources.)

- Earth revolves around the Sun. (Research in encyclopedias or astronomy books; ask knowledgeable people.)
- Dogs walk on four legs. (See for yourself.)

Opinions are statements that cannot be proved. There is no objective evidence you can consult to check the truthfulness of an opinion. Unlike facts, opinions express personal beliefs or judgments. Opinions reveal how someone feels about a subject, not the facts about that subject. You might agree or disagree with someone's opinion, but you cannot prove it right or wrong.

Look at the following opinions. The reasons these statements are classified as opinions appear in parentheses.

- Abraham Lincoln was born to be a president. (You cannot prove this by referring to birth records. There is no evidence to support this belief.)
- Earth is the only planet in our solar system where intelligent life exists. (There is no proof of this. It may be proved true some day, but for now it is just an educated guess—not a fact.)
- The dog is a human's best friend. (This is not a fact; your best friend might not be a dog.)

As you read, be aware that facts and opinions are often mixed together. Both are useful to you as a reader. But to evaluate what you read and to read intelligently, you need to know the difference between the two.

Keeping Events in Order

Sequence, or chronological order, is the order of events in a story or an article or the order of steps in a process. Paying attention to the sequence of events or steps will help you follow what is happening, predict what might happen next, and make sense of a passage.

To make the sequence as clear as possible, writers often use signal words to help the reader get a more exact idea of when things happen. Following is a list of frequently used signal words and phrases:

until	first
next	then
before	after
finally	later
when	while
during	now
at the end	by the time
as soon as	in the beginning

Signal words and phrases are also useful when a writer chooses to relate details or events out of sequence. You need to pay careful attention to determine the correct chronological order.

Making Correct Inferences

Much of what you read *suggests* more than it *says*. Writers often do not state ideas directly in a text. They can't. Think of the time and space it would take to state every idea. And think of how boring that would be! Instead, writers leave it to you, the reader, to fill in the information they leave out—to make inferences. You do this by combining clues in the story or article with knowledge from your own experience.

You make many inferences every day. Suppose, for example, that you are visiting a friend's house for the first time. You see a bag of kitty litter. You infer (make an inference) that the family has a cat. Another day you overhear a conversation. You catch the names of two actors and the words *scene, dialogue,* and *directing*. You infer that the people are discussing a movie or play.

In these situations and others like them, you infer unstated information from what you observe or read. Readers must make inferences in order to understand text.

Be careful about the inferences you make. One set of facts may suggest several inferences. Some of these inferences could be faulty. A correct inference must be supported by evidence.

Remember that bag of kitty litter that caused you to infer that your friend has a cat? That could be a faulty inference. Perhaps your friend's family uses the kitty litter on their icy sidewalks to create traction. To be sure your inference is correct, you need more evidence.

Understanding Main Ideas

The main idea is the most important idea in a paragraph or passage—the idea that provides purpose and direction. The rest of the selection explains, develops, or supports the main idea. Without a main idea, there would be only a collection of unconnected thoughts.

In the following paragraph, the main idea is printed in italics. As you read, observe how the other sentences develop or explain the main idea.

> *Typhoon Chris hit with full fury today on the central coast of Japan.* Heavy rain from the storm flooded the area. High waves carried many homes into the sea. People now fear that the heavy rains will cause mudslides in the central part of the country. The number of people killed by the storm may climb past the 200 mark by Saturday.

In this paragraph, the main idea statement appears first. It is followed by sentences that explain, support, or give details. Sometimes the main idea appears at the end of a paragraph. Writers often put the main idea at the end of a paragraph when their purpose is to persuade or convince. Readers may be more open to a new idea if the reasons for it are presented first.

As you read the following paragraph, think about the overall impact of the supporting ideas. Their purpose is to persuade the reader that the main idea in the last sentence should be accepted.

> Last week there was a head-on collision at Huntington and Canton streets. Just a month ago a pedestrian was struck there. Fortunately, she was only slightly injured. In the past year, there have been more accidents there than at any other corner in the city. In fact, nearly 10 percent of

> all accidents in the city occur at the corner. This intersection is very dangerous, and a traffic signal should be installed there before a life is lost.

The details in the paragraph progress from least important to most important. They achieve their full effect in the main idea statement at the end.

In many cases, the main idea is not expressed in a single sentence. The reader is called upon to interpret all of the ideas expressed in the paragraph and to decide upon a main idea. Read the following paragraph.

> The American author Jack London was once a pupil at the Cole Grammar School in Oakland, California. Each morning the class sang a song. When the teacher noticed that Jack wouldn't sing, she sent him to the principal. He returned to class with a note. The note said that Jack could be excused from singing with the class if he would write an essay every morning.

In this paragraph, the reader has to interpret the individual ideas and to decide on a main idea. This main idea seems reasonable: Jack London's career as a writer began with a punishment in grammar school.

Understanding the concept of the main idea and knowing how to find it is important. Transferring that understanding to your reading and study is also important.

Working Through a Lesson

Part A

1. **Preview the article.** Locate the timed selection in Part A of the lesson that you are going to read. Wait for your teacher's signal to preview. You will have 20 seconds for previewing. Follow the previewing steps described on page 2.
2. **Read the article.** When your teacher gives you the signal, begin reading. Read carefully so that you will be able to answer questions about what you have read. When you finish reading, look at the board and note your reading time. Write this time at the bottom of the page on the line labeled Reading Time.
3. **Complete the exercises.** Answer the 10 questions that follow the article. There are 5 fact questions and 5 idea questions. Choose the best answer to each question and put an X in that box.
4. **Correct your work.** Use the Answer Key at the back of the book to check your answers. Circle any wrong answer and put an X in the box you should have marked. Record the number of correct answers on the appropriate line at the end of the lesson.

Part B

1. **Preview and read the passage.** Use the same techniques you

used to read Part A. Think about what you are reading.

2. **Complete the exercises.** Instructions are given for answering each category of question. There are 15 responses for you to record.

3. **Correct your work.** Use the Answer Key at the back of the book. Circle any wrong answer and write the correct letter or number next to it. Record the number of correct answers on the appropriate line at the end of the lesson.

Plotting Your Progress

1. **Find your reading rate.** Turn to the Reading Rate graph on page 76. Put an X at the point where the vertical line that represents the lesson intersects your reading time, shown along the left-hand side. The right-hand side of the graph will reveal your words-per-minute reading speed.

2. **Find your comprehension score.** Add your scores for Part A and Part B to determine your total number of correct answers. Turn to the Comprehension Score graph on page 77. Put an X at the point where the vertical line that represents your lesson intersects your total correct answers, shown along the left-hand side. The right-hand side of the graph will show the percentage of questions you answered correctly.

3. **Complete the Comprehension Skills Profile.** Turn to page 78. Record your incorrect answers for the Part B exercises. The five Part B skills are listed along the bottom. There are five columns of boxes, one column for each question. For every incorrect answer, put an X in a box for that skill.

To get the most benefit from these lessons, you need to take charge of your own progress in improving your reading speed and comprehension. Studying these graphs will help you to see whether your reading rate is increasing and to determine what skills you need to work on. Your teacher will also review the graphs to check your progress.

To the Teacher

About the Series

Timed Readings Plus in Mathematics includes five books at reading levels 4–8, with one book at each level. Book One contains material at a fourth-grade reading level; Book Two at a fifth-grade level, and so on. The readability level is determined by the New Dale-Chall Readability Formula and is not to be confused with grade or age level of the student. The books are designed for use with students at middle school level and above.

The purposes of the series are as follows:

- to provide systematic, structured reading practice that helps students improve their reading rate and comprehension skills
- to give students practice in reading and understanding informational articles in the content area of mathematics
- to give students experience in reading various text types—informational, expository, narrative, and prescriptive
- to prepare students for taking standardized tests that include timed reading passages in various content areas
- to provide materials with a wide range of reading levels so that students can continue to practice and improve their reading rate and comprehension skills

Because the books are designed for use with students at designated reading levels rather than in a particular grade, the mathematics topics in this series are not correlated to any grade-level curriculum. Most standardized tests require students to read and comprehend mathematics passages. This series provides an opportunity for students to become familiar with the particular requirements of reading mathematics. For example, the vocabulary in a mathematics article is important. Students need to know certain words in order to understand the concepts and the information.

Each book in the series contains 15 two-part lessons. Part A focuses on improving reading rate. This section of the lesson consists of a 400-word timed informational article on a mathematics topic followed by two multiple-choice exercises. Recalling Facts includes five fact questions; Understanding Ideas includes five critical thinking questions.

Part B concentrates on building mastery in critical areas of comprehension. This section consists of a nontimed passage—the "plus" passage—followed by five exercises that address five major comprehension skills. The passage varies in length; its subject matter relates to the content of the timed selection.

Timed Reading and Comprehension

Timed reading is the best-known method of improving reading speed. There is no point in someone's reading at an accelerated speed if the person does not understand what she or he is reading. Nothing is more important than comprehension in reading. The main purpose of reading is to gain knowledge and insight, to understand the information that the writer and the text are communicating.

Few students will be able to read a passage once and answer all of the questions correctly. A score of 70 or 80 percent correct is normal. If the student gets 90 or 100 percent correct, he or she is either reading too slowly or the material is at too low a reading level. A comprehension or critical thinking score of less than 70 percent indicates a need for improvement.

One method of improving comprehension and critical thinking skills is for the student to go back and study each incorrect answer. First, the student should reread the question carefully. It is surprising how many students get the wrong answer simply because they have not read the question carefully. Then the student should look back in the passage to find the place where the question is answered, reread that part of the passage, and think about how to arrive at the correct answer. It is important to be able to recognize a correct answer when it is embedded in the text. Teacher guidance or class discussion will help the student find an answer.

Speed Versus Comprehension

It is not unusual for comprehension scores to decline as reading rate increases during the early weeks of timed readings. If this happens, students should attempt to level off their speed—but not lower it—and concentrate more on comprehension. Usually, if students maintain the higher speed and concentrate on comprehension, scores will gradually improve and within a week or two be back up to normal levels of 70 to 80 percent.

It is important to achieve a proper balance between speed and comprehension. An inefficient reader typically reads everything at one speed, usually slowly. Some poor readers, however, read rapidly but without satisfactory comprehension. The practice that this series provides enables students to increase their reading speed while maintaining normal levels of comprehension.

Getting Started

As a rule, the passages in a book designed to improve reading speed should be relatively easy. The student should not have much difficulty with the vocabulary or the subject matter. Don't worry about the passages being too easy; students should see how quickly and efficiently they can read a passage.

Begin by assigning students to a level. A student should start with a book that is one level below his or her current reading level. If a student's reading level is not known, a suitable starting point would be one or two levels below the student's present grade in school.

Introduce students to the contents and format of the book they are using. Examine the book to see how it is organized. Talk about the parts of each lesson. Discuss the purpose of timed reading and the use of the progress graphs at the back of the book.

Timing the Reading

One suggestion for timing the reading is to have all students begin reading the selection at the same time. After one minute, write on the board the time that has elapsed and begin updating it at 10-second intervals (1:00, 1:10, 1:20, etc.). Another option is to have individual students time themselves with a stopwatch.

Teaching a Lesson

Part A

1. Give students the signal to begin previewing the lesson. Allow 20 seconds, and then discuss special terms or vocabulary that students found.
2. Use one of the methods previously described to time students as they read the passage. (Include the 20-second preview time as part of the first minute.) Tell students to write down the last time shown on the board or the stopwatch when they finish reading. Have them record the time in the designated space after the passage.
3. Next, have students complete the exercises in Part A. Work with them to check their answers, using the Answer Key that begins on page 74. Have them circle incorrect answers, mark the correct answers, and then record the number of correct answers for Part A on the appropriate line at the end of the lesson. Correct responses to eight or more questions indicate satisfactory comprehension and recall.

Part B

1. Have students read the Part B passage and complete the exercises that follow it. Directions are provided with each exercise. Correct responses require deliberation and discrimination.
2. Work with students to check their answers. Then discuss the answers with them and have them record the number of correct answers for Part B at the end of the lesson.

Have students study the correct answers to the questions they answered incorrectly. It is important that they understand why a particular answer is correct or incorrect. Have them reread relevant parts of a passage to clarify an answer. An effective cooperative activity is to have students work in pairs to discuss their answers, explain why they chose the answers they did, and try to resolve differences.

Monitoring Progress

Have students find their total correct answers for the lesson and record their reading time and scores on the graphs on pages 76 and 77. Then have them complete the Comprehension Skills Profile on page 78. For each incorrect response to a question in Part B, students should mark an X in the box above each question type.

The legend on the Reading Rate graph automatically converts reading times to words-per-minute rates. The Comprehension Score graph automatically converts the raw scores to percentages.

These graphs provide a visual record of a student's progress. This record gives the student and you an opportunity to evaluate the student's progress and to determine the types of exercises and skills he or she needs to concentrate on.

Diagnosis and Evaluation

The following are typical reading rates.

Slow Reader—150 Words Per Minute

Average Reader—250 Words Per Minute

Fast Reader—350 Words Per Minute

A student who consistently reads at an average or above-average rate (with satisfactory comprehension) is ready to advance to the next book in the series.

A column of X's in the Comprehension Skills Profile indicates a specific comprehension weakness. Using the profile, you can assess trends in student performance and suggest remedial work if necessary.

1 A Finding Your Car's Gas Mileage

How often will your family stop for gas while driving on a trip? If you know your automobile's gas mileage, you can find the answer. Gas mileage is the total number of miles your car will travel on one gallon of gas. The farther you can travel on one tank of gas, the higher your gas mileage is.

Many factors can affect a car's gas mileage. Larger automobiles usually get lower gas mileage than smaller cars do because they are heavier and require larger engines. A large automobile filled with passengers will get even lower gas mileage. Small, fast sports cars with bigger engines tend to use more gas and have lower gas mileage than other small cars do.

How and where a car is driven affect gas mileage as well. City driving often involves lots of stopping and starting and sitting in stalled traffic. This kind of driving can increase the amount of gas a car uses, lowering its gas mileage. Driving a car up many tall hills can also lower its gas mileage. In most cases, cars will have higher gas mileage when traveling on highways and at a steady speed than when traveling on city streets or hilly roads. Cars that are regularly serviced get better gas mileage too. Cars with well-inflated tires get better mileage as well.

To calculate your car's gas mileage, you must know two things. First, how many gallons does your car's gas tank hold? Second, how many miles can your car travel on a full tank of gas? Your car's odometer shows how many miles the car has traveled. It is usually located near the speedometer on the car's dashboard.

Let's say your car's odometer reading was 8,450 miles when you last filled the tank, and it was 8,930 miles when the gas gauge was on empty. If you subtract 8,450 from 8,930, you find that your car traveled 480 miles on one tank of gas. Now let's say that the gas tank in your car holds 20 gallons of gas. You now have everything you need to find the gas mileage. Divide the 480 miles traveled by the 20 gallons of gas. Your car's gas mileage is 24 miles per gallon.

What if your car's gas tank holds 25 gallons of gas instead? The gas mileage would be lower. A trip of 480 miles divided by 25 gallons of gas is 19.2 miles per gallon.

Reading Time _______

Recalling Facts

1. Gas mileage is
   - ❑ a. the number of miles a car will travel on one tank of gas.
   - ❑ b. the number of gallons a car's gas tank holds.
   - ❑ c. the number of miles a car will travel on one gallon of gas.

2. To figure out a car's gas mileage, you must know
   - ❑ a. the size of the car's gas tank and the miles driven on one full tank of gas.
   - ❑ b. the number of miles driven on one full tank of gas.
   - ❑ c. how much the car weighs and the number of miles driven.

3. The odometer on a car
   - ❑ a. measures the size of the car's gas tank.
   - ❑ b. measures the number of miles the car has traveled.
   - ❑ c. measures how much gas remains in the tank.

4. Gas mileage is calculated by dividing ______ by the number of gallons used.
   - ❑ a. the cost of a full tank of gas
   - ❑ b. the number of gallons in a full tank of gas
   - ❑ c. the number of miles traveled

5. Driving a car in the city will
   - ❑ a. usually raise the car's gas mileage.
   - ❑ b. usually lower the car's gas mileage.
   - ❑ c. not affect the car's gas mileage.

Understanding Ideas

6. One might infer from this reading that
   - ❑ a. driving in city traffic increases gas mileage.
   - ❑ b. driving on open, flat highways decreases gas mileage.
   - ❑ c. driving on icy roads decreases gas mileage.

7. It is likely that a pickup truck will have
   - ❑ a. a higher gas mileage than a small car.
   - ❑ b. a lower gas mileage than a small car.
   - ❑ c. about the same gas mileage as a large, heavy truck.

8. One can conclude that if two different types of cars have the same-size gas tank, then
   - ❑ a. both cars can travel the same distance on one tank of gas.
   - ❑ b. the car with the heaviest load can travel farther on one tank of gas.
   - ❑ c. the car driving at a steady speed can travel farther on one tank of gas than the car in stop-and-go traffic.

9. Probably the simplest way to maintain high gas mileage for a car is to
   - ❑ a. check the tire pressure once a week.
   - ❑ b. drive the same route every day.
   - ❑ c. keep the car free of any heavy objects.

10. Regularly servicing a car probably means
    - ❑ a. keeping the gas tank near full.
    - ❑ b. keeping the engine running well.
    - ❑ c. keeping the tires fully inflated.

1 B Choosing a New Car

Robert and Gosha want to buy a new car, but they cannot decide which kind of car to buy. "We need a car that's safe and also large enough for our growing family," Gosha says. "I'd like one that gets good gas mileage," Robert says. Both want a car that's affordable, one that doesn't cost too much money. They agree to choose between a minivan and a station wagon.

The next day, Robert and Gosha go to see their friend Sofia, who sells cars. "The station wagon costs $23,015," says Sofia. "It gets 19 miles per gallon in the city and 25 on the highway. The minivan is $27,245. It gets 16 miles per gallon in the city and 23 on the highway. The station wagon has a higher safety rating. Both can hold your large family, but the minivan has more room. We are offering a $3,000 rebate on the minivan." Sofia reminds them that a rebate is like a refund.

Robert and Gosha decide on the station wagon. "It costs $1,230 less than the minivan after the rebate. And it has a higher safety rating," says Gosha. "It doesn't have as much room as the minivan, but it does get a little better gas mileage."

1. Recognizing Words in Context

Find the word *refund* in the passage. One definition below is closest to the meaning of that word. One definition has the opposite or nearly the opposite meaning. The remaining definition has a completely different meaning. Label the definitions C for *closest*, O for *opposite or nearly opposite*, and D for *different.*

_______ a. money back

_______ b. agreement

_______ c. extra cost

2. Distinguishing Fact from Opinion

Two of the statements below present *facts,* which can be proved. The other statement is an *opinion,* which expresses someone's thoughts or beliefs. Label the statements F for *fact* and O for *opinion.*

_______ a. The station wagon costs less than the minivan.

_______ b. The station wagon looks better than the minivan.

_______ c. The station wagon has a better safety rating than the minivan.

3. **Keeping Events in Order**

Number the statements below 1, 2, and 3 to show the order in which the events took place.

_____ a. Robert and Gosha decide to buy the station wagon.

_____ b. Robert and Gosha agree to choose between a minivan and a station wagon.

_____ c. Robert and Gosha talk to their friend Sofia.

4. **Making Correct Inferences**

Two of the statements below are correct *inferences,* or reasonable guesses. They are based on information in the passage. The other statement is an incorrect, or faulty, inference. Label the statements C for *correct* inference and F for *faulty* inference.

_____ a. Robert and Gosha think the minivan costs too much.

_____ b. Robert and Gosha's old car is too small for their growing family.

_____ c. Robert and Gosha think gas mileage is more important than price.

5. **Understanding Main Ideas**

One of the statements below expresses the main idea of the passage. One statement is too general, or too broad. The other explains only part of the passage; it is too narrow. Label the statements M for *main idea,* B for *too broad,* and N for *too narrow.*

_____ a. There are many sizes and varieties of cars to choose from.

_____ b. Robert and Gosha consider several of their needs when shopping for a new car.

_____ c. Both the station wagon and the minivan can hold a large family.

Correct Answers, Part A _____

Correct Answers, Part B _____

Total Correct Answers _____

2 A Comparing Temperature Scales

How warm is it today? The answer to that question can be found by checking the temperature on an outdoor thermometer. Temperature can be measured using several kinds of scales. One is called the Fahrenheit scale, named after Daniel Fahrenheit, the man who invented it. Another is called the Celsius, or centigrade, scale. *Centigrade* means "100 degrees." The Celsius scale was named after its inventor, Anders Celsius. Both scales use degrees, or steps of equal size, for measuring temperature. The two scales use very different methods, however.

A degree symbol (°) and the abbreviation for the temperature scale are often used to show temperature. On the Fahrenheit scale, the freezing point of water is 32 degrees Fahrenheit (32°F). The boiling point of water is marked at 212°F. The normal human body temperature is 98.6°F. The Fahrenheit scale is used only in the United States.

On the Celsius scale the freezing point of water is zero degrees (0°C). Water begins to boil at 100°C. The normal human body temperature is 37°C. The Celsius scale was first used in Sweden and France almost 250 years ago. It is commonly used today.

The Kelvin temperature scale (K) was developed by Lord Kelvin in the mid-1800s. The zero point of this scale is equal to –273.15°C (–459.67°F). This zero point is the lowest possible temperature of anything in the universe. Therefore, the Kelvin scale is also known as the "absolute temperature scale." At the freezing point of water, the Kelvin scale reads 273.15K. At the boiling point of water, it reads 373.15K. The Kelvin scale is widely used by scientists, but it is rarely used in daily life.

Imagine it's a warm summer day and you see a sign that says the temperature is 25°C. How do you find the Fahrenheit temperature? You know that the Celsius scale uses 100 degrees to span the change between freezing and boiling. The Fahrenheit scale uses 180 degrees (32 through 212). You can find the relationship of Celsius degrees to Fahrenheit degrees by multiplying the Celsius figure by 1.8 ($180 \div 100$). Then add 32 degrees because the freezing point in Fahrenheit is 32 degrees higher than it is in Celsius. Your computations, then, are $25 \times 1.8 = 45$; $45 + 32 = 77$. You have found that 25°C is the same as 77°F.

Reading Time ______

Recalling Facts

1. The Celsius scale is also called the
   - ❑ a. Fahrenheit scale.
   - ❑ b. centigrade scale.
   - ❑ c. U.S. scale.

2. On the Celsius scale, water freezes at
   - ❑ a. 32°C.
   - ❑ b. 37°C.
   - ❑ c. 0°C.

3. On the Celsius scale, water boils at
   - ❑ a. 32°C.
   - ❑ b. 100°C.
   - ❑ c. 0°C.

4. On the Fahrenheit scale, water freezes at
   - ❑ a. 0°F.
   - ❑ b. 10°F.
   - ❑ c. 32°F.

5. On the Fahrenheit scale, water boils at
   - ❑ a. 100°F.
   - ❑ b. 112°F.
   - ❑ c. 212°F.

Understanding Ideas

6. One can conclude from this passage that
   - ❑ a. the Kelvin scale is used by scientists.
   - ❑ b. the Celsius scale is not scientific.
   - ❑ c. the Fahrenheit scale is most often used in science.

7. A temperature of 20°C is
   - ❑ a. warmer than 20°F.
   - ❑ b. colder than 20°F.
   - ❑ c. the same as 20°F.

8. To convert a reading in Celsius to Fahrenheit, multiply the ______ degrees by 1.8 and add 32 degrees.
   - ❑ a. Celsius
   - ❑ b. Fahrenheit
   - ❑ c. Kelvin

9. The zero point of the Kelvin scale is
   - ❑ a. hotter than the freezing point of water.
   - ❑ b. colder than the freezing point of water.
   - ❑ c. the same as 0°C.

10. Which of the following is *not* a reason why scientists prefer the Kelvin scale to the others?
    - ❑ a. There are 100 degrees between the freezing point of water and the boiling point of water.
    - ❑ b. Its zero point is the lowest temperature in the universe.
    - ❑ c. It can be used to measure temperatures in space.

2 B Daniel Fahrenheit's Thermometer

Whether you are counting money or years, the number 100 is a common point for change. It would seem to be a logical reading on a temperature scale for the boiling point of water. Why, then, did Daniel Fahrenheit set the freezing point of water at 32 degrees and the boiling point at 212 degrees?

When Fahrenheit began his experiments in temperature, he used a mixture of salt and water. That mixture froze at a point he set as 0 on his scale. He decided to use temperature intervals of 12 degrees each. He may have used 12 instead of 10 because 12 is more easily divided by other whole numbers (2, 3, 4, 6). Fahrenheit went on to find that the normal body temperature could be set at the end of 8 of his 12-degree intervals ($12 \times 8 = 96$), that is, at 96 degrees.

Fahrenheit completed his thermometer using the degree intervals he had set. He found that the boiling point of water was 212 degrees. Then he experimented with unsalted water. He found the freezing point of pure water to be at 32 degrees on his thermometer. Later it was found that his reading for body temperature was wrong. That reading was changed to 98.6 degrees.

1. **Recognizing Words in Context**

   Find the word *logical* in the passage. One definition below is closest to the meaning of that word. One definition has the opposite or nearly the opposite meaning. The remaining definition has a completely different meaning. Label the definitions C for *closest,* O for *opposite or nearly opposite,* and D for *different.*

   ______ a. sensible

   ______ b. foolish

   ______ c. awkward

2. **Distinguishing Fact from Opinion**

   Two of the statements below present *facts,* which can be proved. The other statement is an *opinion,* which expresses someone's thoughts or beliefs. Label the statements F for *fact* and O for *opinion.*

   ______ a. Fahrenheit set up his thermometer in intervals of 12 degrees.

   ______ b. The Celsius thermometer is the better temperature scale.

   ______ c. Fahrenheit's first reading for normal body temperature was slightly incorrect.

3. Keeping Events in Order

Number the statements below 1, 2, and 3 to show the order in which the events took place.

_____ a. Fahrenheit found the boiling point of water.

_____ b. Fahrenheit found the freezing point of pure water.

_____ c. Fahrenheit found the freezing point of salt water.

4. Making Correct Inferences

Two of the statements below are correct *inferences,* or reasonable guesses. They are based on information in the passage. The other statement is an incorrect, or faulty, inference. Label the statements C for *correct* inference and F for *faulty* inference.

_____ a. Fahrenheit thought a temperature scale of 0 to 100 would not work.

_____ b. Fahrenheit believed 12-degrees intervals would be easy for people to use.

_____ c. When Fahrenheit set his first reading for body temperature, he believed he was correct.

5. Understanding Main Ideas

One of the statements below expresses the main idea of the passage. One statement is too general, or too broad. The other explains only part of the passage; it is too narrow. Label the statements M for *main idea,* B for *too broad,* and N for *too narrow.*

_____ a. The boiling point of water on the Fahrenheit scale is 212°F.

_____ b. Fahrenheit's experiments with water led him to develop a temperature scale.

_____ c. Fahrenheit was a scientist who was interested in temperature.

Correct Answers, Part A _____

Correct Answers, Part B _____

Total Correct Answers _____

3 A Percentages in Everyday Life

A percentage is a part of a whole. Percentages are fractions with the denominator 100. But instead of using the fraction $^{90}/_{100}$, for example, we just use the symbol %, as in 90%. In fact, the word *percent* means "of 100." If you get 90 answers correct in an exam that has 100 questions, your score is 90 percent (90%).

Imagine you need to wash 40 windows. After a while, you see that you've finished eight of them. What percentage have you completed? To figure percentage, you begin with the numbers you know and make a comparison to 100. Therefore, you would figure that eight windows is to 40 windows as X percent is to 100 percent. To find the number X, work with the known numbers. First multiply 8 times 100, which is 800. Then divide 800 by the other known number (40). You've washed 20 percent of the windows.

Shopping for almost any product often involves percentages. For example, the label on a department store blouse may be marked as "65% cotton, 35% silk." Food labels and packages show the percentage of the recommended daily amount of proteins, vitamins, and other basic elements provided by the food. Many soda and water bottles are made from a percentage of recycled plastic goods, just as many paper products contain a percentage of recycled paper.

Let's say that you and your friends decide to go to the mall. You have the money you made from washing windows. You find a leather coat that is marked 30 percent off the regular price. The original price was $90. You need to know how much money you would save if you buy this coat. Begin with the known numbers. The savings is 30 percent. Think of the formula as 30 percent is to 100 percent as X dollars is to 90 dollars. First multiply the known numbers (30 × 90), which comes to 2,700. Then divide this product by 100. The difference is 27. Your savings is $27. When you subtract this amount from $90, the sale price is $63.

The store charges sales tax on purchases. This tax is a percentage too. If the tax is 6 percent on your $63 purchase, your tax is $3.78 (6 × $63 = $378, and $378 ÷ 100 = $3.78).

Later, you and your friends go to a restaurant. The bill for three sandwiches is $14.40. Your friends turn to you to calculate the 15 percent tip. No problem, right?

Reading Time _______

Recalling Facts

1. Percentage is
   - ❑ a. a number that is stated in tenths.
   - ❑ b. a part of a whole number presented in hundredths.
   - ❑ c. a number higher than 100.

2. The word *percent* means
   - ❑ a. "of a cent."
   - ❑ b. "of part."
   - ❑ c. "of 100."

3. An item that is on sale at 30 percent off is ______ than the original cost.
   - ❑ a. 70 percent less
   - ❑ b. 30 percent less
   - ❑ c. 40 percent less

4. Sales tax is ______ of an item.
   - ❑ a. included in the sale price
   - ❑ b. a percentage of the sale price
   - ❑ c. a percentage of the original cost

5. To find a percentage, first begin with the numbers you know and
   - ❑ a. make a comparison to 100.
   - ❑ b. multiply by 100.
   - ❑ c. divide by 100.

Understanding Ideas

6. If a pair of shoes is marked 20 percent off the regular price and you pay $80, the original cost is
   - ❑ a. $60.
   - ❑ b. $120.
   - ❑ c. $100.

7. A quick way to divide by 100 is to move the decimal point to the left by the number of zeros, so
   - ❑ a. $378 ÷ 100 = $3.78.
   - ❑ b. $378 ÷ 100 = $378.
   - ❑ c. $378 ÷ 100 = $37.80.

8. In order to find out what percentage of muffins at a bake sale were sold,
   - ❑ a. find out how many muffins were baked.
   - ❑ b. find out how many muffins were sold.
   - ❑ c. find out both the number of muffins baked and the number sold.

9. If 40 out of 50 questions are answered correctly on a test, the test score is
   - ❑ a. 80 percent.
   - ❑ b. 40 percent.
   - ❑ c. 90 percent.

10. If a sign says "buy two for the price of one," the amount of savings is
    - ❑ a. 50 cents.
    - ❑ b. 100 percent.
    - ❑ c. 50 percent.

3 B Levon's Challenge

At the end of the last school year, Levon and his dad took an extended look at Levon's test scores. Levon knew how to calculate an average for a set of numbers: Add the figures together, and then divide the sum by the number of figures that were added.

Levon had scored 73, 87, 80, and 84 percent on four math tests. The sum of the four test scores added together was 324. His average, then, was 81 percent (324 divided by 4). His scores on four English tests were 88, 80, 86, and 82 percent. The sum of the four test scores added together was 336. So his average was 84 percent. Levon's social studies and science test averages were 92 and 71 percent.

Next they wanted to know the average of all the test scores. Levon had taken the same number of tests in each subject, so they added the math, English, social studies, and science test averages together and divided by 4. The average of all his test scores last year was 82 percent.

They could see that the science test scores were bringing down the total test score average. Levon's father offered a deal to his son. "Raise your average test scores," he said, "and I will raise your allowance."

1. **Recognizing Words in Context**

   Find the word *extended* in the passage. One definition below is closest to the meaning of that word. One definition has the opposite or nearly the opposite meaning. The remaining definition has a completely different meaning. Label the definitions C for *closest,* O for *opposite or nearly opposite,* and D for *different.*

   ______ a. long

   ______ b. quick

   ______ c. angry

2. **Distinguishing Fact from Opinion**

   Two of the statements below present *facts,* which can be proved. The other statement is an *opinion,* which expresses someone's thoughts or beliefs. Label the statements F for *fact* and O for *opinion.*

   ______ a. Levon took fewer math tests than English tests.

   ______ b. Levon didn't study enough in science class.

   ______ c. Levon's science test scores were the lowest of all his test scores.

3. Keeping Events in Order

Number the statements below 1, 2, and 3 to show the order in which the events took place.

_____ a. Levon calculated that all his test scores for the year averaged 82 percent.

_____ b. Levon calculated the average of his math test scores.

_____ c. Levon's dad offered a deal to his son.

4. Making Correct Inferences

Two of the statements below are correct *inferences,* or reasonable guesses. They are based on information in the passage. The other statement is an incorrect, or faulty, inference. Label the statements C for *correct* inference and F for *faulty* inference.

_____ a. Levon has to study harder in science class next year.

_____ b. Levon's dad is expecting Levon to raise his average test scores.

_____ c. If Levon had taken fewer science tests, his average would have been better.

5. Understanding Main Ideas

One of the statements below expresses the main idea of the passage. One statement is too general, or too broad. The other explains only part of the passage; it is too narrow. Label the statements M for *main idea,* B for *too broad,* and N for *too narrow.*

_____ a. Levon and his dad figured out his average test scores to see where he needed improvement.

_____ b. Higher test scores mean higher averages.

_____ c. Levon knew how to calculate an average.

Correct Answers, Part A _____

Correct Answers, Part B _____

Total Correct Answers _____

4 A Using a Road Map

Maps are interesting as well as useful. Most maps are representations of Earth's surface. Mapmakers show the relationship between the distances on the map and real distances on Earth by providing a map scale. This relationship is expressed as a ratio. A map of a town might have a ratio of 1:100,000. This means that one inch on the map equals 100,000 inches on Earth. You can find how many miles 100,000 inches are when you know that there are 63,360 inches in a mile. So 100,000 ÷ 63,360 = 1.58 miles. In other words, one inch on the map represents 1.58 miles on Earth.

There are small-scale maps and large-scale maps. A small-scale map shows a large area with a small amount of detail. A large-scale map shows a small area with a large amount of detail. One way to understand this is to imagine you are floating in a balloon just above your hometown. As you look down, the ratio of the area you see might be expressed as 1:10,000. As the balloon rises, the details become smaller, and the scale also becomes smaller. An example of a small-scale map is a map with the ratio 1:1,000,000.

Road maps, like many other maps, show the distance in miles between places. Road maps are large-scale maps. However, road maps usually do not show the large-number ratio of one inch to thousands or hundreds of thousands of inches. They often show only the smaller ratio, one inch to miles.

Now let's use a map scale on a road map to find out the distance from your home to the state capital. You find your town and the capital on the map and see that a single direct road connects them. The scale shows that 1 inch = 25 miles. Measuring the distance on the map between your town and the capital, you find they are seven inches apart. The state capital, then, is 175 miles from your home.

Along the way is Centerville, a little less than two inches from your town, or about 40 miles away. You have to pick up a new soccer jersey there. To calculate the amount of time it takes to travel to Centerville, you need to know your travel speed as well as the number of miles you need to travel. The speed limit is 55 miles per hour. If you travel at that speed, you should be in Centerville in about 45 minutes.

Reading Time _______

Recalling Facts

1. A map scale
   - ❑ a. shows the relationship between the distances on the map and the real distances on Earth.
   - ❑ b. is a representation of Earth's surface.
   - ❑ c. shows the distance in miles between places.

2. A small-scale map shows
   - ❑ a. a large area with a small amount of detail.
   - ❑ b. how big Earth is.
   - ❑ c. a small area with a large amount of detail.

3. A map ratio of 1:750,000 means that
   - ❑ a. 1 inch equals 750,000 miles.
   - ❑ b. 1 inch equals 750,000 inches.
   - ❑ c. 1 inch equals 750 miles.

4. How many inches are there in a mile?
   - ❑ a. 63,360
   - ❑ b. 1.58
   - ❑ c. 100,000

5. To find the time it takes to travel a certain number of miles, you need to know
   - ❑ a. the time and the number of miles to you need to travel.
   - ❑ b. the travel speed and the number of miles to travel.
   - ❑ c. the speed limit as well as the number of miles to travel.

Understanding Ideas

6. A ratio is
   - ❑ a. the relationship in amount, number, or size between two or more things.
   - ❑ b. a number that expresses amount.
   - ❑ c. the difference between scales.

7. A map with the scale ratio 1:10,000,000 is an example of a
   - ❑ a. medium-scale map.
   - ❑ b. large-scale map.
   - ❑ c. small-scale map.

8. A scale ratio of 1:10,000 represents ______ miles per inch than a ratio of 1:1,000.
   - ❑ a. more
   - ❑ b. fewer
   - ❑ c. the same number of

9. A small-scale map is good for
   - ❑ a. finding the route to a place 15 miles away.
   - ❑ b. finding the nearest park.
   - ❑ c. locating an island in the Pacific Ocean.

10. If the scale on your road map reads "1 inch: 20 miles" and on the map the city you want to visit is six inches from your home,
    - ❑ a. you must travel 120 miles to get to the city.
    - ❑ b. you must travel 20 miles to get to the city.
    - ❑ c. you must travel 60 miles to get to the city.

4 B Are We There Yet?

Kim and Hector wanted to visit friends across the state. Kim purchased a road map to help them find the shortest route and to figure out how many miles they had to travel.

Hector remembered a trip he had taken to Aurora State Park. He had gotten there by the shortest route he could find on his map. But many of the roads had low speed limits. His total travel time was almost two hours longer than he thought it would be. Going home, he took a route that was 25 miles longer on the map, but his trip was almost an hour shorter.

Along with their map, Hector and Kim decided to use a mileage chart to plan their trip across the state. A mileage chart shows the shortest distance between selected cities. Kim made a list of the cities they would pass through along their way. Next, Hector found the distance from their starting point to the first city along the route. Then he found the distance from that city to the next one on the route. Finally, he added all of the distances together. They now knew the shortest route and the total number of miles to their destination.

1. Recognizing Words in Context

Find the word *destination* in the passage. One definition below is closest to the meaning of that word. One definition has the opposite or nearly the opposite meaning. The remaining definition has a completely different meaning. Label the definitions C for *closest,* O for *opposite or nearly opposite,* and D for *different.*

______ a. goal

______ b. beginning

______ c. travel

2. Distinguishing Fact from Opinion

Two of the statements below present *facts,* which can be proved. The other statement is an *opinion,* which expresses someone's thoughts or beliefs. Label the statements F for *fact* and O for *opinion.*

______ a. A map shows the shortest route between places.

______ b. A mileage chart shows the shortest distance between places.

______ c. Hector and Kim should have taken a train or flown instead.

3. Keeping Events in Order

Number the statements below 1, 2, and 3 to show the order in which the events took place.

_____ a. Hector and Kim decided to take a trip.

_____ b. Hector shared his story of traveling to Aurora State Park.

_____ c. Kim made a list of the cities they would pass through along their way.

4. Making Correct Inferences

Two of the statements below are correct *inferences,* or reasonable guesses. They are based on information in the passage. The other statement is an incorrect, or faulty, inference. Label the statements C for *correct* inference and F for *faulty* inference.

_____ a. Hector thought his route to the state park was the shortest possible route.

_____ b. The map Kim purchased would show the shortest route and the total miles.

_____ c. The mileage chart would not show the route they would take.

5. Understanding Main Ideas

One of the statements below expresses the main idea of the passage. One statement is too general, or too broad. The other explains only part of the passage; it is too narrow. Label the statements M for *main idea,* B for *too broad,* and N for *too narrow.*

_____ a. Kim and Hector used a mileage chart with their road map to plan the route for a trip.

_____ b. Hector and Kim wanted to visit friends across the state.

_____ c. A map and a mileage chart can be used to plan a trip.

Correct Answers, Part A _____

Correct Answers, Part B _____

Total Correct Answers _____

5 A Shopping for the Best Value

Careful grocery shoppers may have difficulty making a "quick trip" to the market. They often need to take time finding the best value for their money. They wonder whether they should buy the large can or the small can. They think about which product tastes better. If you're looking for the best value, you need to compare items. To compare means to look at how one item measures up against others.

When you compare prices, be sure that the quantity, or amount of each item, is the same. If the quantity is different, you might not choose the best value. Items such as milk and orange juice are sold in various units of measure. Gallons, quarts, pints, and ounces are four of the most common units of measure. Each pint holds 16 ounces. Each quart holds two pints. And each gallon holds four quarts. When comparing items of different quantities, you must consider the price per unit of measure.

For example, milk is often sold in gallons, half gallons, and quarts. A gallon of White Star milk costs $2.99. A half gallon costs $1.79. And a quart costs $1.19. Which is the better value? At first it may seem that the quart and half gallon are better values because they are cheaper than the gallon. To compare prices, however, remember to compare the same amount of each product. Two individual quarts of milk cost $2.38 ($1.19 × 2). That means the half gallon is a better value than the two quarts. Two half gallons of milk, which equal one full gallon, cost $3.58 ($1.79 × 2). The gallon of milk at $2.99 is cheaper by $0.59. Usually, larger quantities are cheaper per unit than smaller quantities.

So should you always buy the largest quantity of an item? If your family cannot drink a gallon of milk in a week, the milk may spoil. In cases like this, buying the smaller quantity at a higher price per unit may be the better choice. You may feel that Blue Circle milk tastes better than White Star milk. However, a gallon of Blue Circle milk costs $3.69. You might buy Blue Circle because, for you, that is a better value. Buying the largest quantity or the cheapest brand may not always be the best choice. When you consider all of your choices, you can make the best decision about the value of a product.

Reading Time ______

Recalling Facts

1. When looking for the best value, a shopper needs to
   - ❑ a. look for the largest quantity.
   - ❑ b. find the cheapest brand.
   - ❑ c. compare items.
2. When comparing items, it is important to make sure
   - ❑ a. the quantities of the items are the same.
   - ❑ b. the product brands are the same.
   - ❑ c. the prices of the items are the same.
3. Comparing a half gallon of White Star milk with a gallon of the same brand shows that
   - ❑ a. the half gallon has the cheaper price per unit.
   - ❑ b. the half gallon has the most quantity.
   - ❑ c. the gallon has the cheaper price per unit.
4. Buying the largest quantity or cheapest brand is
   - ❑ a. not always the best choice.
   - ❑ b. always the best choice.
   - ❑ c. never the best choice.
5. One gallon is the same quantity as
   - ❑ a. four quarts.
   - ❑ b. two quarts.
   - ❑ c. six quarts.

Understanding Ideas

6. One can conclude from the information in this passage that
   - ❑ a. items that cost more taste better.
   - ❑ b. a good value is not the same for all people.
   - ❑ c. people who shop for value always pay less for groceries.
7. Gallons, quarts, pints, and ounces are units of
   - ❑ a. measurement.
   - ❑ b. cost.
   - ❑ c. price.
8. The way to find whether an item is the best value is to
   - ❑ a. consider the brand names.
   - ❑ b. consider the cost.
   - ❑ c. compare it with similar items.
9. One can infer from the passage that the best value can be found by comparing
   - ❑ a. two items rather than three items.
   - ❑ b. three items rather than two items.
   - ❑ c. larger items rather than smaller items.
10. It is most likely that four individual quarts of paint
    - ❑ a. will cost more than a gallon of the same paint.
    - ❑ b. are a better value than a gallon of the same paint.
    - ❑ c. will cost less than a gallon of the same paint.

5 B Comparing Breakfast Cereals

Rudy wanted to buy a healthful cereal for his children. He also needed to find the best value for the money. He chose rice, bran, and wheat with raisins for his comparison.

"The rice cereal has the highest amount of vitamin A but less calcium than the other two," Rudy thought. "The wheat with raisins has the highest amount of all other vitamins." He continued comparing. The rice cereal has 3 percent of the recommended daily amount of fiber. The bran has four times as much fiber (12 percent), but the wheat with raisins cereal has more than six times as much (20 percent).

The wheat with raisins cereal comes in a 24-ounce box and costs $4.79. The bran cereal is in an 18-ounce box for $4.29. The rice cereal, in an 18-ounce box, is the least expensive at $2.88. That means the wheat with raisins cereal is 20 cents per ounce (4.79 divided by 24). The bran cereal is 24 cents an ounce (4.29 divided by 18). And the rice cereal is 16 cents an ounce (2.88 divided by 18).

"I'll buy two boxes of wheat with raisins cereal," Rudy thought. "It's not the cheapest, but it has the highest vitamin content."

1. Recognizing Words in Context

Find the word *recommended* in the passage. One definition below is closest to the meaning of that word. One definition has the opposite or nearly the opposite meaning. The remaining definition has a completely different meaning. Label the definitions C for *closest,* O for *opposite or nearly opposite,* and D for *different.*

_____ a. provided

_____ b. advised

_____ c. warned against

2. Distinguishing Fact from Opinion

Two of the statements below present *facts,* which can be proved. The other statement is an *opinion,* which expresses someone's thoughts or beliefs. Label the statements F for *fact* and O for *opinion.*

_____ a. In Rudy's comparison, the rice cereal had the cheapest price per unit.

_____ b. Rudy thought that the wheat with raisins cereal had the most vitamins.

_____ c. Bran cereal does not taste as good as wheat with raisins cereal.

3. Keeping Events in Order

Number the statements below 1, 2, and 3 to show the order in which the events took place.

_____ a. Rudy compared the prices of the cereals.

_____ b. Rudy chose the wheat with raisins cereal.

_____ c. Rudy compared the vitamins in the cereals.

4. Making Correct Inferences

Two of the statements below are correct *inferences,* or reasonable guesses. They are based on information in the passage. The other statement is an incorrect, or faulty, inference. Label the statements C for *correct* inference and F for *faulty* inference.

_____ a. Rudy thought all three cereals were healthful.

_____ b. Rudy's children would have liked the less expensive rice cereal just as well.

_____ c. A 24-ounce box of cereal will last longer than an 18-ounce box.

5. Understanding Main Ideas

One of the statements below expresses the main idea of the passage. One statement is too general, or too broad. The other explains only part of the passage; it is too narrow. Label the statements M for *main idea,* B for *too broad,* and N for *too narrow.*

_____ a. There are many different ways to shop for food.

_____ b. Some cereals have more vitamins than others do.

_____ c. After comparing prices and healthfulness, Rudy chose the cereal with the best value.

Correct Answers, Part A _____

Correct Answers, Part B _____

Total Correct Answers _____

6 A Catering an Event

People who want to host a social event, such as a sales meeting or a birthday party, sometimes hire caterers to provide food and services. Caterers are businesses that prepare and serve food for events. Some caterers also provide music, gifts, and decorations.

Caterers need to ask several questions to learn what services are needed. How many guests will attend the event? What kind of food should be served, and how much food will be needed? Will the guests be served from a buffet, or will waiters serve the food at the guests' tables? What sort of beverages will be served?

People who hire caterers usually decide on a budget, or a plan to use a certain amount of money, for the entire event. To do this, they must find out what the caterer charges for the items they want. Then they must plan carefully and make adjustments so that the total cost fits within the budget.

In this example, Apex Wrenches wants to host a conference and hire Candy's Catering to serve lunch. The guests will be 250 new salespeople. Apex also wants Candy's to provide small key chain wrenches as gifts to each of the lunch guests. Apex sets the budget for the event at \$5,000 (250 × \$20).

Candy's charges \$20 a person for lunch, so the meals will cost \$5,000. There will be no money left for the gifts, which cost \$300. Apex and Candy's must work together to make a few changes in the plans. Candy's tells Apex that the charge for a buffet-style lunch is only \$12 a person, or a total of \$3,000 (250 × \$12). The cost is less because Candy's would not have to pay as many waiters to serve lunch. Apex agrees to the change and learns that Candy's charges an additional \$5 a person for a selection of desserts, or a total of \$1,250 (250 × \$5). Apex adds the desserts to the menu because the total cost of the desserts, the buffet, and the gifts comes to \$4,550. There is \$450 left in the budget.

Candy's has to think about its budget too. It has to buy the food and purchase special containers to carry it to the event. Candy's also has to buy and maintain vans to deliver the food. Cooks must be paid to make the food, and waiters must be hired to serve the food. Candy's figures out how much of these costs can be added to the price of its services.

Reading Time _______

Recalling Facts

1. A caterer is
   - ❑ a. a business that provides food and services for social events.
   - ❑ b. a business that plans special events.
   - ❑ c. a chef who prepares food for large parties.

2. People who hire caterers usually
   - ❑ a. ask what type of food the guests will be served.
   - ❑ b. charge the caterer for the items they want.
   - ❑ c. prefer to set a budget, or an estimated cost, for the entire event.

3. A budget is
   - ❑ a. the least amount of money that can be spent.
   - ❑ b. a plan to use a certain amount of money.
   - ❑ c. the total cost of a planned party.

4. The budget did not allow for Candy's Caterers to provide both
   - ❑ a. gift key chain wrenches and a buffet-style lunch.
   - ❑ b. a buffet lunch and a choice of desserts.
   - ❑ c. waiters to serve lunch and gift key chain wrenches.

5. A caterer's budget costs include money
   - ❑ a. for the waiters' uniforms.
   - ❑ b. for gifts to hand out.
   - ❑ c. to hire waiters to serve food.

Understanding Ideas

6. One might conclude from the passage that
   - ❑ a. the caterer's budget is not as important as the client's budget.
   - ❑ b. it is important to decide on a budget when planning an event.
   - ❑ c. it is best to change the budget when the plans don't work out.

7. "Working within a budget" usually involves
   - ❑ a. spending more money than the budget allows.
   - ❑ b. adding more money to the budget.
   - ❑ c. making changes to cut costs.

8. It is likely that Candy's Caterers noticed the extra $450 in the budget and suggested
   - ❑ a. $450 worth of extra services.
   - ❑ b. that it split the amount with Apex.
   - ❑ c. that Apex give the money as a tip.

9. According to the passage, which of these statements is most likely true?
   - ❑ a. The Candy's Catering budget for this event did not change.
   - ❑ b. Apex's salespeople would have preferred waiter service to buffet service.
   - ❑ c. Apex's budget for this event was based on similar company events.

10. It can be assumed that Candy's pays its waiters
    - ❑ a. from the money it charges for their services.
    - ❑ b. according to the type of service provided.
    - ❑ c. more than it pays its cooks.

6 B

Rachel's Bat Mitzvah: The Costs and Arrangements

Rachel's 12th birthday is coming up soon. She'll celebrate her bat mitzvah, an important rite in a Jewish girl's life. Many Jewish girls celebrate their bat mitzvah with traditional prayers and practices. And often there is also a celebration party!

Rachel's parents have planned to spend $1,000 on the bat mitzvah, the same amount they spent on her older brother's bar mitzvah. The party will be held in the family's backyard.

Her mother has ordered two fancy sheet cakes, enough for 100 people. Rachel will honor her mother, grandmothers, and aunts by lighting candles on the cakes. The cakes cost $100 each. For entertainment, Rachel's cousins will play traditional dance music. They will be paid $250. The family has arranged to spend $400 on food and beverages.

Rachel found a beautiful party dress for $125, but buying it would leave only $25 for some decorations she really wants. Then Rachel's mother discovered that they had forgotten to add in the cost of plates, forks, knives, and spoons. There are three choices. Rachel's parents can contribute more money to the amount they had set aside for the party. Or they can cut back and have less music or food or fewer guests. Or Rachel can buy a less expensive dress.

1. Recognizing Words in Context

Find the word *rite* in the passage. One definition below is closest to the meaning of that word. One definition has the opposite or nearly the opposite meaning. The remaining definition has a completely different meaning. Label the definitions C for *closest,* O for *opposite or nearly opposite,* and D for *different.*

_____ a. informal event

_____ b. ceremony

_____ c. request

2. Distinguishing Fact from Opinion

Two of the statements below present *facts,* which can be proved. The other statement is an *opinion,* which expresses someone's thoughts or beliefs. Label the statements F for *fact* and O for *opinion.*

_____ a. Rachel is planning to honor the women in her family.

_____ b. Rachel's friends and relatives will enjoy the dance music.

_____ c. Rachel has an older brother.

3. Keeping Events in Order

Number the statements below 1, 2, and 3 to show the order in which the events took place.

______ a. Rachel's mother remembers to include the cost of plates, forks, knives, and spoons.

______ b. Rachel turns 12.

______ c. Rachel finds a beautiful party dress.

4. Making Correct Inferences

Two of the statements below are correct *inferences,* or reasonable guesses. They are based on information in the passage. The other statement is an incorrect, or faulty, inference. Label the statements C for *correct* inference and F for *faulty* inference.

______ a. Rachel's parents will not cut back on the traditional celebrations.

______ b. For many Jewish girls, turning 12 is an important event.

______ c. Rachel's parents are not too concerned about how much money they will spend on the bat mitzvah.

5. Understanding Main Ideas

One of the statements below expresses the main idea of the passage. One statement is too general, or too broad. The other explains only part of the passage; it is too narrow. Label the statements M for *main idea,* B for *too broad,* and N for *too narrow.*

______ a. There are many costs to consider when planning for a party.

______ b. Rachel's bat mitzvah will include traditional and religious practices.

______ c. Rachel's parents plan a party to celebrate their daughter's bat mitzvah.

Correct Answers, Part A ______

Correct Answers, Part B ______

Total Correct Answers ______

7 A Small-World Theory

Each year Ben is glad when Martin Luther King Jr. Day gives him a day off from school. Ben knows that this day honors an important man, but Ben doesn't feel connected to him. In a sense, however, Ben really is linked to Dr. King through the "small-world theory." Ben's mom (0) has a stepfather (1) whose uncle (2) once met and spoke to Eleanor Mondale (3), the daughter of former Vice President Walter Mondale (4), who knew Dr. King (5). In a way, Ben is only "five people away" from Martin Luther King Jr.

The small-world theory says that everyone in the world is connected through a short chain of people they know. This chain is known as *degrees of separation*. There are zero degrees of separation between you and the people you know directly. So there are zero degrees between Ben and his mom. There is one degree of separation when just one person separates you from someone you don't know. So Ben's mom's stepfather is one degree away from Ben. As the chain continues, the stepfather's uncle is two degrees, Eleanor Mondale is three degrees, her father is four degrees, and Dr. King is five degrees away from Ben. The theory goes on to say that there are no more than six degrees of separation between any two people in the world.

The small-world theory is based on math. The theory assumes that a person knows 100 people and that each one of those people knows 50 different people. Each of those 50 people knows another 50 people, and so on. If the calculation is carried out to six degrees, it multiplies as follows: $100 \times 50 \times 50 \times 50 \times 50 \times 50 = 31.25 \times 10^9$, or more than 31 billion. The world has about 6 billion people. So in theory, six degrees of separation can cover the world.

Does the small-world theory work? It has never been proved. There are questions about how well it can apply in some areas. For example, the theory needs to establish links to remote groups of people. So it may not work in faraway places where everyone knows the people in their village but few know anyone outside it. Also, the theory relies on a few people with huge networks who link the rest of us.

Does the theory matter? Maybe it just makes us all think a little more about our place in the world.

Reading Time _______

Recalling Facts

1. According to the small-world theory, there are no more than ______ degrees of separation between everyone in the world.
   - ❑ a. three
   - ❑ b. six
   - ❑ c. five
2. The number of degrees of separation between you and your best friend is
   - ❑ a. zero.
   - ❑ b. three.
   - ❑ c. six.
3. The number of degrees of separation between you and a friend's friend you haven't met is
   - ❑ a. zero.
   - ❑ b. one.
   - ❑ c. three.
4. Ben is three degrees of separation away from
   - ❑ a. Eleanor Mondale.
   - ❑ b. Dr. Martin Luther King Jr.
   - ❑ c. his mom's dentist.
5. The theory assumes that a person knows
   - ❑ a. six people.
   - ❑ b. 100 people.
   - ❑ c. 50 people.

Understanding Ideas

6. One can conclude from the information in this passage that
   - ❑ a. more research is needed to prove the small-world theory.
   - ❑ b. a star links everyone to famous people.
   - ❑ c. this theory doesn't work.
7. Famous people probably have
   - ❑ a. fewer degrees of separation between them and others.
   - ❑ b. about the same six degrees of separation between them and others.
   - ❑ c. more degrees of separation between them and others.
8. The theory may not work very well with
   - ❑ a. movie stars.
   - ❑ b. politicians.
   - ❑ c. people who live in remote areas.
9. According to the passage, Eleanor Mondale is ______ of separation from Dr. Martin Luther King Jr.
   - ❑ a. one degree
   - ❑ b. two degrees
   - ❑ c. zero degrees
10. If Ben's mother's doctor knows Britney's doctor, then
    - ❑ a. Ben is four degrees away from Britney.
    - ❑ b. Ben's mom is three degrees away from Britney.
    - ❑ c. Ben is three degrees away from Britney.

7 B What Is Chance?

One day Kelly picked up the phone to call Lynn, and there was no dial tone. Then Kelly heard Lynn say, "Hello?" "Lynn?" Kelly said. "I was just going to call you!"

A mysterious coincidence? Not really. The laws of probability account for this happening.

Kelly and Lynn call each other two or three times a day, or about 1,000 times a year. Let's say that the variable N stands for the total number of calls that the two friends make to each other in a year. Now, for purposes of example, let's say that the chance of their calling each other at the same moment is 1 in 1,000 (.001). Let's call that number p. The laws of chance say that Np ($N \times p$) equals the average number of times in a year that they are likely to call each other at the same moment. So if Kelly and Lynn call each other 1,000 times in a year, $1{,}000 \times .001$ equals one call a year. It was mathematically likely to happen sometime.

People calculate odds for fun. A famous example is called the "birthday problem." It states that in any group of 23 people, there's a 50-50 chance that two of them will share a birthday.

1. Recognizing Words in Context

Find the word *probability* in the passage. One definition below is closest to the meaning of that word. One definition has the opposite or nearly the opposite meaning. The remaining definition has a completely different meaning. Label the definitions C for *closest,* O for *opposite or nearly opposite,* and D for *different.*

_____ a. ability to change

_____ b. impossibility

_____ c. chance that something will happen

2. Distinguishing Fact from Opinion

Two of the statements below present *facts,* which can be proved. The other statement is an *opinion,* which expresses someone's thoughts or beliefs. Label the statements F for *fact* and O for *opinion.*

_____ a. Kelly and Lynn talk on the phone too much.

_____ b. Any rare event has some chance of happening.

_____ c. Np equals the average number of times an event is likely to occur.

3. Keeping Events in Order

Number the statements below 1, 2, and 3 to show the order in which the events took place.

_____ a. Lynn said, "Hello?"

_____ b. Kelly heard no dial tone.

_____ c. Kelly picked up the phone.

4. Making Correct Inferences

Two of the statements below are correct *inferences,* or reasonable guesses. They are based on information in the passage. The other statement is an incorrect, or faulty, inference. Label the statements C for *correct* inference and F for *faulty* inference.

_____ a. If something has a 50-50 chance of happening, it is not likely to happen.

_____ b. In a group of 100 people, the chance that two people share a birthday is better than 50-50.

_____ c. Kelly and Lynn enjoy talking to each other.

5. Understanding Main Ideas

One of the statements below expresses the main idea of the passage. One statement is too general, or too broad. The other explains only part of the passage; it is too narrow. Label the statements M for *main idea,* B for *too broad,* and N for *too narrow.*

_____ a. Any rare event has some chance of occurring.

_____ b. *Np* equals the average number of times an event is likely to occur.

_____ c. Coincidences happen according to laws of chance.

Correct Answers, Part A _____

Correct Answers, Part B _____

Total Correct Answers _____

8 A Race Cars—Behind the Speed

Race cars are some of the fastest-moving machines in the world. An Indy-style race car, the kind that races at the Indianapolis 500, can reach speeds above 230 miles per hour. That's faster than many small planes travel when they take off and fly.

Since race cars change direction often, race teams are interested in a car's velocity as well as its speed. *Velocity* is the rate at which something moves in a certain direction. Whereas *speed* also tells us how fast something moves, it tells us nothing about the object's change of position. Distance divided by time equals speed. For instance, if you drive 140 miles in two hours, moving westward, your speed is 70 miles per hour (140 ÷ 2 = 70 mph). However, your velocity is 70 mph *west.*

Let's say that Jenny drove at 70 miles per hour to the next town and then returned home at the same speed. On average, her speed was 70 mph, but her average velocity was 0, because *overall* she did not change her position—she came back to the very point where she started.

One factor that can lower a car's speed and velocity is friction. Friction is a force that slows down motion. As a race car moves, its rolling tires rub against the track, causing friction.

When engineers design race cars, they study the coefficient of friction. This involves considering both the weight of an object and the force needed to move that object. For instance, a 100-pound box may require 20 pounds of force to push it across a floor. To compute the coefficient of friction, the engineer would divide 20 by 100, getting a result of .2. Objects such as oiled machine parts and race car wheels have a much lower coefficient of friction—usually about .002.

The science of aerodynamics studies the ways that air friction affects the motion of objects. As a race car passes through air, forces push against it. People who design race cars study these forces to improve the performance of their cars. Drag is a kind of force produced by air friction that slows the car down. Downward forces help hold the car on the track. The more force holding a car on the track, the faster it can go around corners and through curves. So, designers of race cars try to reduce the car's drag while increasing the downward forces.

Reading Time ______

Recalling Facts

1. Race cars that run in the Indianapolis 500 can reach speeds of more than
   - ❑ a. 200 miles per hour.
   - ❑ b. 185 miles per hour.
   - ❑ c. 230 miles per hour.
2. The rate at which something moves in a given direction is
   - ❑ a. speed.
   - ❑ b. velocity.
   - ❑ c. downward forces.
3. A force that slows down motion is
   - ❑ a. velocity.
   - ❑ b. tires.
   - ❑ c. friction.
4. The science that studies the effects of air on moving objects is called
   - ❑ a. drag forces.
   - ❑ b. aerodynamics.
   - ❑ c. friction.
5. Engineers compute the coefficient of friction by
   - ❑ a. increasing the downward forces.
   - ❑ b. adding the weight of an object and the force needed to move it.
   - ❑ c. dividing the force needed to move an object by the weight of the object.

Understanding Ideas

6. One can conclude from the information in this passage that race car makers
   - ❑ a. have improved aerodynamics as much as possible.
   - ❑ b. will design cars that will go faster.
   - ❑ c. have much more to discover about race car design.
7. It is likely that strong drag forces will
   - ❑ a. cause a race car to go slower.
   - ❑ b. cause a race car to go faster.
   - ❑ c. cause a race car to stop.
8. One can conclude from the information that the coefficient of friction is lower for
   - ❑ a. pushing a desk than pushing a shopping cart.
   - ❑ b. running on sand than swimming in a pool.
   - ❑ c. turning a doorknob than turning an unopened jar lid.
9. A ball rolled across the floor will stop because
   - ❑ a. friction will make it stop rolling.
   - ❑ b. downward forces will push against it.
   - ❑ c. it has not been pushed hard enough.
10. One can infer that without drag, all race cars would move
    - ❑ a. slowly.
    - ❑ b. at speeds much different from one another.
    - ❑ c. much faster than they do.

8 B

Horsepower

Horsepower is a unit of measure that tells you the power of an engine. Horsepower was first used as a unit of measure in the late 18th century by James Watt. Watt built a steam engine that was more powerful than the earlier steam engines. He compared the power of his steam engines to the power of his horses. The measure of the rate of doing work—how fast something can be moved—is called power. The amount of work needed to move one pound of matter the distance of one foot is a foot-pound. A single horsepower equals 550 foot-pounds per second. Three horsepower equals 1,650 foot-pounds per second.

The horsepower of a vehicle engine is not the same as the horsepower driving the vehicle's wheels. A massive truck and a small car might both have a 190-horsepower engine. However, the weight of the truck could mean a loss of 20 percent of its horsepower. The horsepower turning the truck's wheels is only 152 (190 hp × 20% = 38; 190 − 38 = 152). The lightweight car may lose only 10 percent of its horsepower. Its wheels get a higher amount (190 hp × 10% = 19; 190 − 19 = 171).

1. Recognizing Words in Context

Find the word *massive* in the passage. One definition below is closest to the meaning of that word. One definition has the opposite or nearly the opposite meaning. The remaining definition has a completely different meaning. Label the definitions C for *closest*, O for *opposite or nearly opposite*, and D for *different*.

______ a. tiny

______ b. powerful

______ c. large

2. Distinguishing Fact from Opinion

Two of the statements below present *facts*, which can be proved. The other statement is an *opinion*, which expresses someone's thoughts or beliefs. Label the statements F for *fact* and O for *opinion*.

______ a. One horsepower equals 550 foot-pounds per second.

______ b. Power is the measure of the rate of doing some amount of work.

______ c. An engine with 8.0 hp is better than one with 7.0 hp.

3. **Keeping Events in Order**

Number the statements below 1, 2, and 3 to show the order in which the events took place.

______ a. Car engines start to be measured by horsepower.

______ b. Watt constructs his first steam engine.

______ c. Watt compares the power of horses to the power of steam engines.

4. **Making Correct Inferences**

Two of the statements below are correct *inferences,* or reasonable guesses. They are based on information in the passage. The other statement is an incorrect, or faulty, inference. Label the statements C for *correct* inference and F for *faulty* inference.

______ a. The heavier the machine, the more horsepower is needed to move it.

______ b. Machines that do not require speed do not need much horsepower.

______ c. Watt used the horse as a measure of power because horses were a common source of power.

5. **Understanding Main Ideas**

One of the statements below expresses the main idea of the passage. One statement is too general, or too broad. The other explains only part of the passage; it is too narrow. Label the statements M for *main idea,* B for *too broad,* and N for *too narrow.*

______ a. Horsepower was originally used to compare the power of horses to the power of steam engines.

______ b. Horsepower measures the power of different kinds of engines.

______ c. Horsepower is a unit of measure.

Correct Answers, Part A ______

Correct Answers, Part B ______

Total Correct Answers ______

9 A Roman Numerals

The Roman number system was developed by the ancient Romans. Unlike the ancient Greeks, the Romans did not develop theories requiring the use of numbers, such as in geometry and physics. The Romans used their numbers mainly for doing business. Roman numerals were used for keeping records of taxes and trade throughout Rome's great empire.

The Romans used numerals that are the same as some of our letters. The numerals I, V, X, L, C, D, and M stand for 1, 5, 10, 50, 100, 500, and 1,000. For a large number, the single number values are arranged from left to right, beginning with the greatest value and ending with the smallest value. The value of the entire number is then found by adding all of the single number values together. The number MDCLXVI, for example, would be read as 1,000 + 500 + 100 + 50 + 10 + 5 + 1, or 1,666.

Some numbers include the same letter more than once. The number 8 is VIII, formed by adding three ones to V. If numbers with lower values are to the right of a larger number, the lower numbers are added to the larger number. So, the number VIII is 5 + 1 + 1 + 1 = 8.

Except for very large numbers, Romans never used the same numeral more than three times in a row. Instead of writing the number 4 as IIII, subtraction is used. The rule is: If a number with a lower value is to the left of the larger number, then the lower number is subtracted from the larger number. Four is 5 minus 1, or IV. Nine is 10 minus 1, or IX. Forty is 50 minus 10, or XL.

The subtraction feature of Roman numerals may make figuring out the value of some three-letter numbers puzzling. For example, XIX is 19, or 10 + 9. Why isn't XIX 21, or 10 + 1 + 10? Simply stated, the subtraction rule means that IX stands for 9. XIX is therefore 10 (X) plus the smaller number, 9 (IX), that follows, or 19. The numeral for 21 is XXI.

Roman numerals are still used today, but not very often. Roman numerals are often seen carved into a corner of some large buildings to show when the buildings were constructed. Roman numerals are also seen on the faces of clocks and watches and in the first pages of books.

Reading Time ______

Recalling Facts

1. The Roman number system
   - ❑ a. was similar to that of the ancient Greeks.
   - ❑ b. was used with Roman geometry theories.
   - ❑ c. was used for everyday purposes.

2. The values of larger Roman numerals are arranged left to right from
   - ❑ a. lesser to greater.
   - ❑ b. greater to lesser.
   - ❑ c. single-letter to multiple-letter.

3. The value of the Roman numeral MDCLXVI is found by
   - ❑ a. adding all the single number values together.
   - ❑ b. subtracting the values from right to left.
   - ❑ c. counting the larger numbers first and then the smaller numbers.

4. To show the number 40 in Roman numerals, the Romans
   - ❑ a. subtracted 10 from 50.
   - ❑ b. added four 10s.
   - ❑ c. added two 20s.

5. To find the value of the Roman numeral IX,
   - ❑ a. add the larger number to the smaller number.
   - ❑ b. subtract the smaller number from the larger number.
   - ❑ c. subtract the larger number from the smaller number.

Understanding Ideas

6. The best way to describe the Romans in their use of math is
   - ❑ a. businesslike.
   - ❑ b. artistic.
   - ❑ c. proud.

7. One could conclude that the Roman number system was
   - ❑ a. used only in Rome.
   - ❑ b. taught to Romans by the Greeks.
   - ❑ c. used throughout the Roman Empire.

8. In Roman numerals, 89 would be written as
   - ❑ a. LIX.
   - ❑ b. XIX.
   - ❑ c. LXXXIX.

9. In Roman numerals, the year 2004 would be written as
   - ❑ a. MMIV.
   - ❑ b. MDLX.
   - ❑ c. MMIIII.

10. Which of the following statements is *not* true?
    - ❑ a. Addition and subtraction are needed to understand Roman numerals.
    - ❑ b. Roman numerals are occasionally used today.
    - ❑ c. The Roman numeral for zero is 0.

9 B Arabic Numerals and Place-Value

The Arabic numerals 0, 1, 2, 3, 4, 5, 6, 7, 8, and 9 in use today are a clear, easy-to-use set of symbols for counting. The Arabic numerals are based on a number system first used in ancient India. The Arabic number system was the first to use the zero. Before this system, the idea of zero was sometimes shown by using a blank space. This way of doing things, however, often caused confusion. Blank spaces might be forgotten when writing a number or missed when reading a number.

Perhaps the most important feature of Arabic numerals is place-value. Each of the numbers 1 to 9 occupies a single place. Then, once 10 is reached, a second place is begun with 1 and then 0 from left to right. These positions remain the same as we count through 99. At 100, a third place is begun with 1 - 0 - 0 from left to right. These positions remain the same until 999 is reached. Beginning with 1,000, four spaces are used, as 1 - 0 - 0 - 0 fill those spaces from left to right. The practice of place-value helped simplify the process of addition and subtraction as well as multiplication and division.

1. Recognizing Words in Context

Find the word *process* in the passage. One definition below is closest to the meaning of that word. One definition has the opposite or nearly the opposite meaning. The remaining definition has a completely different meaning. Label the definitions C for *closest,* O for *opposite or nearly opposite,* and D for *different.*

______ a. a single step in a plan

______ b. difficulty with a task

______ c. a way of doing something in steps

2. Distinguishing Fact from Opinion

Two of the statements below present *facts,* which can be proved. The other statement is an *opinion,* which expresses someone's thoughts or beliefs. Label the statements F for *fact* and O for *opinion.*

______ a. The Arabic numerals originally came from ancient India.

______ b. The Arabic numerals should always be used in place of Roman numerals.

______ c. Place-value is a feature of Arabic numerals.

3. Keeping Events in Order

Number the statements below 1, 2, and 3 to show the order in which the events took place.

______ a. The ancient Indians began using what are now called Arabic numerals.

______ b. The Arabic number system was the first to use zero.

______ c. A blank space was used in place of a zero.

4. Making Correct Inferences

Two of the statements below are correct *inferences,* or reasonable guesses. They are based on information in the passage. The other statement is an incorrect, or faulty, inference. Label the statements C for *correct* inference and F for *faulty* inference.

______ a. The use of Arabic numbers spread because it was a system that worked well.

______ b. The practice of place-value helped simplify the process of addition and subtraction more than multiplication and division.

______ c. Before the use of place-value, people sometimes could not tell if a blank space was used.

5. Understanding Main Ideas

One of the statements below expresses the main idea of the passage. One statement is too general, or too broad. The other explains only part of the passage; it is too narrow. Label the statements M for *main idea,* B for *too broad,* and N for *too narrow.*

______ a. The number system we use today was developed over many centuries.

______ b. The ancient Indians were the first people to use zero.

______ c. The Arabic number system, with its idea of place-value, simplified basic arithmetic.

Correct Answers, Part A ______

Correct Answers, Part B ______

Total Correct Answers ______

10 A

Consumers and Lenders: The Business of Borrowing Money

People who want to buy an expensive item such as a car will likely need to get a loan. When a consumer wants to buy a house, the long-term loan the buyer will need is called a mortgage. Banks will lend money to people who have paid their bills on time and established good credit. Lenders decide whether they want to lend a customer money by examining the customer's credit history. This is a record of how much money a person owes and how promptly that person has been paying his or her bills.

A lender will also want to know how much a borrower earns each month. This will help the bank decide whether the borrower would be able to repay a loan. For instance, a customer applies for a car loan. The person's monthly take-home pay is $1,200. The customer has monthly credit card payments of $175 and monthly rent payments of $500. That means there is $525 left over for other monthly expenses. The bank needs to decide whether the customer can afford a $260 car payment each month.

Banks and other lenders such as mortgage companies make a profit from lending money. They make money by charging people interest. The amount of interest they charge is called the interest rate. It is a percentage of the loan amount. For example, a customer who gets a $10,000 loan with a 7 percent interest rate will need to pay back a total of $10,700 to the lender. Some banks offer lower interest rates than others. They might do this especially with customers who have strong credit reports. That is because banks believe that people with good credit are more likely to repay a loan than people with poor credit. It is a good idea to look around for the best interest rate available. On a three-year car loan of $10,000, for example, a 7 percent interest rate means a monthly payment about $18 higher than with a 3 percent interest rate.

Banks and other companies that lend money borrow from the Federal Reserve Bank, which decides the rate of interest it will charge other banks. This is called the prime rate. It affects the amount of interest the banks charge. How much a person will have to pay to borrow money depends on three major factors. These are the prime rate, the person's credit history, and competition among lenders.

Reading Time ______

Recalling Facts

1. A loan for a home is called
   - ❑ a. a prime rate.
   - ❑ b. a mortgage.
   - ❑ c. rate of interest.

2. Banks are most likely to loan money to
   - ❑ a. people with a proven record of good credit.
   - ❑ b. people who have borrowed from them before.
   - ❑ c. people who have a mortgage.

3. Banks make a profit from
   - ❑ a. paying interest on savings accounts.
   - ❑ b. selling houses.
   - ❑ c. collecting interest on loans.

4. The prime rate
   - ❑ a. is the interest rate banks offer to customers with good credit.
   - ❑ b. does not affect other interest rates.
   - ❑ c. is set by the Federal Reserve Bank.

5. Which of the following statements is *not* true?
   - ❑ a. The Federal Reserve Bank decides how much money other banks can loan.
   - ❑ b. When the Federal Reserve Bank lowers interest rates, it is really lowering the prime rate.
   - ❑ c. A changing prime rate affects the amount of interest banks will charge.

Understanding Ideas

6. Before it will loan money to a person, a bank will most likely look at the person's
   - ❑ a. credit report.
   - ❑ b. monthly work pay.
   - ❑ c. both of the above.

7. Banks compete with one another by offering
   - ❑ a. lower interest rates on loans.
   - ❑ b. higher interest rates on loans.
   - ❑ c. mortgage loans.

8. A person who wants a good credit history would benefit most from
   - ❑ a. paying monthly bills on time.
   - ❑ b. never buying anything on credit.
   - ❑ c. saving money.

9. You can infer that a $15,000 loan at 10 percent interest will cost ______ a $15,000 loan at 5 percent interest.
   - ❑ a. $1,425 more than
   - ❑ b. $750 more than
   - ❑ c. $1,500 more than

10. One can conclude from the information in this passage that
    - ❑ a. consumers always pay back more for a loan than they borrow.
    - ❑ b. consumers can always choose the amount of interest they want to pay.
    - ❑ c. interest rates don't change very often.

10 B The Terms of a Home Mortgage

There are two common types of mortgage loans. A loan with a variable, or adjustable, rate has an interest rate that may change from year to year. A fixed-rate mortgage loan has an interest rate that stays the same for the entire term of the mortgage.

Mortgages most often have a term of 15 or 30 years. During this time, monthly payments are made on the loan. For a 30-year mortgage, repayment is spread out in 360 payments (12 months × 30 years = 360). In most cases, one would pay less each month on a 30-year mortgage than on a 15-year loan. However, the borrower must pay interest for 30 years. Most banks and mortgage companies offer customers a lower interest rate on a loan with a shorter term.

On a 15-year, fixed-rate home mortgage of $100,000 with an interest rate of 5 percent, the monthly payment would be $790.79. Over 15 years, the borrower would pay $42,342.86 in interest.

Maybe the borrower purchased a home with a 30-year, fixed-rate loan of $100,000 and an interest rate of 5.75 percent. The monthly payment in this case would be only $583.57. However, over 30 years, the borrower would pay $110,086.23 in interest.

1. Recognizing Words in Context

Find the word *repayment* in the passage. One definition below is closest to the meaning of that word. One definition has the opposite or nearly the opposite meaning. The remaining definition has a completely different meaning. Label the definitions C for *closest,* O for *opposite or nearly opposite,* and D for *different.*

_____ a. amount to pay back

_____ b. amount charged

_____ c. amount not owed

2. Distinguishing Fact from Opinion

Two of the statements below present *facts,* which can be proved. The other statement is an *opinion,* which expresses someone's thoughts or beliefs. Label the statements F for *fact* and O for *opinion.*

_____ a. Mortgages most often have a term of 15 or 30 years.

_____ b. A variable mortgage rate has an interest rate that can change over time.

_____ c. A loan with a 15-year variable interest rate is better than one with a 30-year fixed rate.

3. **Keeping Events in Order**

Number the statements below 1, 2, and 3 to show the order in which the events take place.

______ a. Home buyers arrange the terms of the mortgage with the bank.

______ b. Home buyers decide the amount of mortgage payment they can afford each month.

______ c. Home buyers find a house they want to buy.

4. **Making Correct Inferences**

Two of the statements below are correct *inferences,* or reasonable guesses. They are based on information in the passage. The other statement is an incorrect, or faulty, inference. Label the statements C for *correct* inference and F for *faulty* inference.

______ a. People want a 15-year loan rather than a 30-year loan if they want to pay less over time.

______ b. Variable interest rates are not likely to change.

______ c. People want a 30-year loan rather than a 15-year loan if they want lower monthly payments.

5. **Understanding Main Ideas**

One of the statements below expresses the main idea of the passage. One statement is too general, or too broad. The other explains only part of the passage; it is too narrow. Label the statements M for *main idea,* B for *too broad,* and N for *too narrow.*

______ a. There are many important factors to take into account when buying a house.

______ b. A fixed-rate mortgage loan means the interest rate stays the same for the period of the loan.

______ c. There are different types of mortgage loans, so home buyers can find the one that fits their financial needs.

Correct Answers, Part A ______

Correct Answers, Part B ______

Total Correct Answers ______

11 A How Did Our Calendar Develop?

The calendar most often used today is called a solar calendar. *Solar* means "having to do with the sun." The solar calendar is based on the time it takes Earth to travel once around the sun. Earth makes this journey around the sun in 365¼ days. Our calendar has 365 days every three out of four years. To make up for the extra one-quarter day, it has 366 days every fourth year. The four one-quarter days are joined into one day and added to the fourth year, called a leap year. The extra day in a leap year is the 29th day in February.

The solar calendar is not the only way of counting the months. People in earlier times based their calendars on the cycle of the moon. Their months started with the new moon and lasted about 29 days. Calendars based on the moon are called lunar calendars. Lunar calendars are still used.

The solar calendar can be traced back to ancient Rome, about 2,000 years ago. The first Roman calendar had been based on the cycles of the moon. It lasted 304 days and was divided into 10 months, for an average of 30.4 days per month. Then the Roman emperor Julius Caesar made a trip to Egypt, where he learned how the Egyptians measured time. When Caesar returned to Rome, he changed the calendar. Instead of a lunar calendar with 304 days divided into 10 months, he created a 12-month solar calendar with 365 days every three out of four years and a leap year every fourth year.

In 1582 Pope Gregory XIII, with the help of his scientists, made more changes to the solar calendar. It became the calendar that we use today. This calendar became known as the Gregorian calendar. Like the calendar that Caesar created, the Gregorian calendar set the year at 365 days, with a leap year every fourth year. The Gregorian calendar worked better than Caesar's calendar and other earlier calendars. But it was not fully accepted until the 20th century.

Keeping track of the number of days in each month of our solar calendar can be a challenge. Many years ago, the following rhyme was created to help us remember how many days are in each month:

Thirty days have September,
April, June, and November.
All the rest have thirty-one,
Except February the only one
Which leap years change each fourth time
From twenty-eight to twenty-nine.

Reading Time ______

Recalling Facts

1. The calendar most often used today
   - ❑ a. is based on the cycles of the moon.
   - ❑ b. has always been the way it is now.
   - ❑ c. can be traced back to Julius Caesar.

2. The solar calendar we use today is called
   - ❑ a. the Gregorian calendar.
   - ❑ b. the Caesar calendar.
   - ❑ c. the February calendar.

3. Leap years are needed because
   - ❑ a. people can't agree on the number of days in a year.
   - ❑ b. the lunar cycle is 28 days.
   - ❑ c. Earth takes 365¼ days to orbit the sun.

4. Calendars based on the cycle of the moon have months that last about
   - ❑ a. 31 days.
   - ❑ b. 27 days.
   - ❑ c. 29 days.

5. One year in the first Roman calendar was made up of
   - ❑ a. 12 months and 304 days.
   - ❑ b. 10 months and 365 days.
   - ❑ c. 10 months and 304 days.

Understanding Ideas

6. One might infer from this passage that
   - ❑ a. the lunar calendar was more often correct than the solar calendar was.
   - ❑ b. calendars are based on natural cycles.
   - ❑ c. our current calendar will never change.

7. It is likely that the lunar calendar was developed
   - ❑ a. by people whose life and work were closely tied to the cycles of the moon.
   - ❑ b. by astronomers who studied the moon.
   - ❑ c. by Julius Caesar before he adopted the Egyptian calendar.

8. One can infer that the Gregorian calendar was not fully accepted for centuries because
   - ❑ a. people thought the Gregorian calendar was incorrect.
   - ❑ b. people did not like Pope Gregory.
   - ❑ c. people did not want to change.

9. The only months with 30 days are
   - ❑ a. September, October, and November.
   - ❑ b. April, June, September, and November.
   - ❑ c. March, June, and September.

10. It is likely that the solar calendar is based on
    - ❑ a. the cycle of the moon.
    - ❑ b. the cycle of the seasons.
    - ❑ c. both of the above.

11 B The Chinese Calendar

The Chinese calendar shares features of both the solar and lunar calendars. It is called a "lunisolar" calendar. The Chinese calendar is usually made up of 12 months. Each month corresponds to the phases of the lunar cycle. The solar year is 12 months and about 365¼ days. The lunar cycle is completed in about 29½ days. So, a 12-month lunar year will be about $12 \times 29.5 = 354$ days, or about 11 days shorter than a solar year.

A leap month is added about every third year to keep the Chinese calendar in tune with the seasons. A complete cycle of this calendar takes 60 years. This period is divided into five cycles of 12 years each.

The Chinese calendar is used for setting the dates of traditional festivals, such as the Chinese New Year. The Chinese New Year begins on the first day of the Chinese calendar and lasts for 15 days. The Chinese New Year celebrates the beginning of spring. The beginning of the Chinese year always falls between January 21 and February 21 on the Gregorian calendar.

1. Recognizing Words in Context

Find the word *corresponds* in the passage. One definition below is closest to the meaning of that word. One definition has the opposite or nearly the opposite meaning. The remaining definition has a completely different meaning. Label the definitions C for *closest,* O for *opposite or nearly opposite,* and D for *different.*

______ a. changes

______ b. differs

______ c. relates

2. Distinguishing Fact from Opinion

Two of the statements below present *facts,* which can be proved. The other statement is an *opinion,* which expresses someone's thoughts or beliefs. Label the statements F for *fact* and O for *opinion.*

______ a. The Chinese calendar is called a lunisolar calendar.

______ b. The Chinese calendar should be based on a solar calendar.

______ c. The Chinese New Year lasts 15 days.

3. Keeping Events in Order

Two of the statements below describe events that happen at the same time. The other statement describes an event that happens before or after those events. Label them S for *same time,* B for *before,* and A for *after.*

______ a. The Chinese New Year celebrates the beginning of spring.

______ b. Traditional Chinese festivals take place during the year.

______ c. The Chinese New Year lasts 15 days.

4. Making Correct Inferences

Two of the statements below are correct *inferences,* or reasonable guesses. They are based on information in the passage. The other statement is an incorrect, or faulty, inference. Label the statements C for *correct* inference and F for *faulty* inference.

______ a. The Chinese cannot tell in advance on what day the New Year will arrive.

______ b. The Chinese New Year is also a spring festival.

______ c. The Chinese New Year begins on a different day each year according to the Gregorian calendar.

5. Understanding Main Ideas

One of the statements below expresses the main idea of the passage. One statement is too general, or too broad. The other explains only part of the passage; it is too narrow. Label the statements M for *main idea,* B for *too broad,* and N for *too narrow.*

______ a. The Chinese calendar has an interesting history.

______ b. The Chinese calendar often includes an extra month.

______ c. The Chinese calendar, which changes each year, is used for setting the dates of traditional festivals.

Correct Answers, Part A ______

Correct Answers, Part B ______

Total Correct Answers ______

12 A The Pyramids of Egypt

The Great Pyramid is called one of the Seven Wonders of the Ancient World. It was built for the pharaoh Khufu, a leader of the Egyptian people. He was buried in a room at the heart of the pyramid. The stones of the room fit together so well that a card could not pass between them. The Great Pyramid is more than 4,500 years old. It is the oldest of the Seven Wonders and the only one that still stands.

To build the Great Pyramid, the Egyptians needed to measure a square base, with four right angles. The pyramid's base has been found to be level within a margin of 2.1 centimeters, less than 1 inch. The base covers about 13 acres and is 751 feet long on each side. The four corners of the base point exactly to the north, south, east, and west.

More than 2.3 million blocks were carved from limestone and granite and then pulled, pushed, and dragged for miles to the building site. The average weight of each block was about 2.5 tons, or about 5,000 pounds. Some of the blocks weighed as much as 16 tons, or 32,000 pounds. It took the Egyptians about 20 years to complete the Great Pyramid.

A major problem facing the builders of the Great Pyramid was getting the large stone blocks into place. Most people agree on the method the Egyptians used to achieve this. It is believed that they built ramps laid upon inclined planes made of brick and rubble. The ramps were slicked with water and mud. The workers would then push and drag the blocks up the slippery ramps. Eventually, as the pyramid grew taller, the ramps, and the inclined planes that supported the ramps, had to be made longer. The base of the inclined plane had to be widened also, or else it would have collapsed under the great weight.

The Great Pyramid was 481 feet high when it was finished. The Egyptians themselves had no tools for measuring the height of the pyramid. The Greek mathematician Thales, while visiting at the time, showed the Egyptians how to measure the height of a pyramid. He waited for the time of day when his shadow's length equaled his own height. From his knowledge of mathematics, Thales knew that at this same moment, the length of the pyramid's shadow must also equal the pyramid's height. So Thales simply measured the pyramid's shadow.

Reading Time ______

Recalling Facts

1. The Great Pyramid is
   - ❑ a. where the pharaoh Khufu was buried.
   - ❑ b. a temple for the pharaoh.
   - ❑ c. the tallest structure in the world.

2. The Great Pyramid was built in Egypt about
   - ❑ a. 400 years ago.
   - ❑ b. 40,000 years ago.
   - ❑ c. 4,500 years ago.

3. The pyramid's square base is level within a margin of
   - ❑ a. less than 1 inch.
   - ❑ b. 1.2 centimeters.
   - ❑ c. 2.1 inches.

4. The stone blocks were raised into place on the pyramid wall
   - ❑ a. by a system of ramps and inclined planes.
   - ❑ b. by a system of ropes and sleds.
   - ❑ c. by a system of carts and levers.

5. Thales knew the height of the pyramid because
   - ❑ a. it was the same as the length of the pyramid's shadow.
   - ❑ b. it was longer than the length of his own shadow.
   - ❑ c. the sun always casts a shadow that is longer than the object.

Understanding Ideas

6. One might infer that the Egyptians
   - ❑ a. found the four right angles of the base by accident.
   - ❑ b. knew how much each stone weighed.
   - ❑ c. improved their building methods over many years.

7. The ramps and the supporting inclined planes were longest
   - ❑ a. in the later stages of building.
   - ❑ b. the middle stages of building.
   - ❑ c. in the early stages of building.

8. Which of the following is *not* true about the inclined planes used by the Egyptians?
   - ❑ a. They kept the ramps from being crushed by the weight of the stones.
   - ❑ b. They supported the angles of the ramp.
   - ❑ c. They were made slick to aid the movement of the stones.

9. From the context of the passage, one can infer that a square
   - ❑ a. has four equal sides.
   - ❑ b. points exactly to north, south, east, and west.
   - ❑ c. is level to within an inch.

10. Another way to measure the height of the pyramid, if it were possible, would have been to
    - ❑ a. measure from the top to the center of the base.
    - ❑ b. measure around the base.
    - ❑ c. measure a side.

12 B Measuring the Surface Area of a Pyramid

A pyramid such as the Great Pyramid in Egypt is a three-dimensional solid. The base is a polygon, and the sides are triangles that meet at a point called the apex. The surface area of a pyramid is the sum of the area of the base and all the sides. How would we measure the surface area of the Great Pyramid? We know that its base is a square because it has four right angles, and each side of the base measures 751 feet in length. So, we can use the formula for finding the area of a square: length (751 feet) × width (751 feet) = 564,001 square feet.

How do we find the area of the four sides? You'll have to picture in your mind the Great Pyramid. The sides of a pyramid with a square base are identical triangles. The formula for finding the area of a triangle is one-half of the base multiplied by the height. Half the base of a triangle on one side of the Great Pyramid is 375.5 feet (751 ÷ 2). The height of that triangle is about 610 feet. So, 375.5 feet × 610 feet = 229,055 square feet.

Finally, add the area of the base (564,001 square feet) to the sum of the areas of all sides (229,055 square feet × 4), and the surface area is 1,480,221 square feet.

The surface area of the Great Pyramid today is less than it was when it was new, because the rock face has been worn down by the weather.

1. Recognizing Words in Context

Find the word *apex* in the passage. One definition below is closest to the meaning of that word. One definition has the opposite or nearly the opposite meaning. The remaining definition has a completely different meaning. Label the definitions C for *closest,* O for *opposite or nearly opposite,* and D for *different.*

_____ a. peak

_____ b. base

_____ c. angle

2. Distinguishing Fact from Opinion

Two of the statements below present *facts,* which can be proved. The other statement is an *opinion,* which expresses someone's thoughts or beliefs. Label the statements F for *fact* and O for *opinion.*

_____ a. The base of the Great Pyramid is a square.

_____ b. The Great Pyramid will not last much longer.

_____ c. The sides of a pyramid with a square base are identical triangles.

3. Keeping Events in Order

Number the steps below 1, 2, and 3 to show the order of the steps as described in the passage.

______ a. Find the area of one of the triangular sides.

______ b. Add the area of all four sides to the area of the base.

______ c. Measure the area of the base.

4. Making Correct Inferences

Two of the statements below are correct *inferences,* or reasonable guesses. They are based on information in the passage. The other statement is an incorrect, or faulty, inference. Label the statements C for *correct* inference and F for *faulty* inference.

______ a. Rain and wind have worn away the Great Pyramid.

______ b. A square is a four-sided polygon.

______ c. The Great Pyramid is taller than its base is wide.

5. Understanding Main Ideas

One of the statements below expresses the main idea of the passage. One statement is too general, or too broad. The other explains only part of the passage; it is too narrow. Label the statements M for *main idea,* B for *too broad,* and N for *too narrow.*

______ a. The surface area of a pyramid with a square base may be found by adding the area of its four sides to the area of its base.

______ b. A pyramid is made up of a base that is a polygon and sides that are triangles.

______ c. Surface area is the sum of the areas of the exposed sides of an object.

Correct Answers, Part A ______

Correct Answers, Part B ______

Total Correct Answers ______

13 A Measuring Circles

Geometry is a branch of mathematics that studies points, lines, planes, and figures, including circles. Everywhere you look, you can see examples of circles.

All points on a circle are the same distance from the center of the circle. In other words, a true circle is perfectly round. You can draw a line from the center of a circle to any point on the circle. The distance from the center to that point is called the radius.

The distance around a circle is called the circumference. The word *circumference* comes from the Latin word *circum,* meaning "around." A circle contains 360 degrees. A semicircle is half a circle, so it contains 180 degrees. The diameter is a line that starts from any point on a circle, goes through the center, and ends on the exact opposite side of the circle. So a diameter equals two radii. When two or more diameters are drawn from different points on a circle, they form angles. When you slice a round pizza, you usually slice along several diameters. If you slice a pizza into eight equal pieces, each piece will have a 45-degree angle.

We can use circles to measure other things. Each time your bicycle wheel rolls around once, you know how far you have traveled if you know the wheel's circumference. The same principle is used in the mileage counter of a car.

A compass is an instrument used for drawing circles. This compass is different from the compass that shows direction. It has two legs connected by a pivot. One leg has a pointed end that holds the compass in place on a piece of paper, and the other leg holds a pencil. As you turn the compass, the pencil will trace a circle.

The distance around a circle is about three times the length of the diameter. This is true for all circles. If you divide the circumference by the diameter, you will get a number that is approximately 3.14. This is the value that is often used for the number known as pi, or π. The full value for pi cannot be written down, since it goes on forever to the right of the decimal point. Pi is always the same number, no matter how large the circle.

Reading Time ______

Recalling Facts

1. The distance around a circle is
   - ❑ a. the diameter.
   - ❑ b. pi.
   - ❑ c. the circumference.

2. The word *circumference* is derived from the Latin word *circum*, meaning
   - ❑ a. through.
   - ❑ b. around.
   - ❑ c. perimeter.

3. Which of the following statements is *not* true?
   - ❑ a. The distance around a circle is about three times the distance across the circle.
   - ❑ b. The diameter is the distance around a circle.
   - ❑ c. A circle contains 360 degrees.

4. The distance from the center of a circle to any point on the circle is called
   - ❑ a. the diameter.
   - ❑ b. the circumference.
   - ❑ c. the radius.

5. The distance around a circle is about ______ times the distance across the circle.
   - ❑ a. four
   - ❑ b. two
   - ❑ c. three

Understanding Ideas

6. Compasses are used for
   - ❑ a. drawing exact circles.
   - ❑ b. finding the diameter of a circle.
   - ❑ c. finding the radius of a circle.

7. If a round pizza is sliced into four equal pieces, each piece will form an angle equal to ______ degrees.
   - ❑ a. 180
   - ❑ b. 90
   - ❑ c. 45

8. The radius
   - ❑ a. is the distance around the circle.
   - ❑ b. connects the center of the circle to any point on the circle.
   - ❑ c. divides the circle in half.

9. When ______ diameters are drawn through a circle at right angles to each other, the angles created in the circle are 90 degrees.
   - ❑ a. six
   - ❑ b. four
   - ❑ c. two

10. A person facing north will have made a 180-degree turn when he or she
    - ❑ a. turns around one full turn.
    - ❑ b. turns and faces east.
    - ❑ c. turns and faces south.

13 B Let's Have Some Wheel Fun

For thousands of years, people have used the wheel as an aid for moving themselves or other objects. Wheels are used for work and for recreation. An example of a fun wheel is the Ferris wheel. This amusement park ride is basically a large circle with passenger seats attached to it. People riding in the seats travel the entire circumference of the wheel as it turns around and around.

The Ferris wheel was introduced at the World's Fair of 1893, in Chicago, Illinois. It was built by George Ferris, who got the idea from looking at merry-go-rounds. Ferris believed that a vertical wheel could be as much fun as a horizontal wheel, if not more fun.

The diameter of the original Ferris wheel was 250 feet—making it the largest wheel in the world at the time. The circumference was 785 feet. Thirty-six wooden cars held about 60 riders each. More than 2,000 people could ride the wheel at one time.

Ferris wheels are divided by many spokes, as on a bicycle. The spokes running across the wheel through the center form many angles. The number of angles depends on the number of spokes on the wheel.

1. Recognizing Words in Context

Find the word *recreation* in the passage. One definition below is closest to the meaning of that word. One definition has the opposite or nearly the opposite meaning. The remaining definition has a completely different meaning. Label the definitions C for *closest,* O for *opposite or nearly opposite,* and D for *different.*

_____ a. moving

_____ b. labor

_____ c. play

2. Distinguishing Fact from Opinion

Two of the statements below present *facts,* which can be proved. The other statement is an *opinion,* which expresses someone's thoughts or beliefs. Label the statements F for *fact* and O for *opinion.*

_____ a. George Ferris's wheel was the largest in the world in 1893.

_____ b. The diameter of the original Ferris wheel was 250 feet.

_____ c. The Ferris wheel was the best ride at the 1893 World's Fair.

3. Keeping Events in Order

Number the statements below 1, 2, and 3 to show the order in which the events took place.

______ a. George Ferris built his wheel.

______ b. George Ferris got the idea for his wheel from the merry-go-round.

______ c. The Ferris wheel was introduced at the 1893 World's Fair.

4. Making Correct Inferences

Two of the statements below are correct *inferences,* or reasonable guesses. They are based on information in the passage. The other statement is an incorrect, or faulty, inference. Label the statements C for *correct* inference and F for *faulty* inference.

______ a. Ferris believed that people would enjoy his vertical wheel because of its height.

______ b. The spokes on Ferris wheels are there to make the wheel look like a bicycle wheel.

______ c. Bigger Ferris wheels have been built since 1893.

5. Understanding Main Ideas

One of the statements below expresses the main idea of the passage. One statement is too general, or too broad. The other explains only part of the passage; it is too narrow. Label the statements M for *main idea,* B for *too broad,* and N for *too narrow.*

______ a. The Ferris wheel is an example of a circle that is used for fun.

______ b. Wheels are objects in the shape of a circle and have many uses.

______ c. Like bicycle wheels, Ferris wheels are divided by spokes.

Correct Answers, Part A ______

Correct Answers, Part B ______

Total Correct Answers ______

14 A Distances and Light-Years in Space

Astronomy is the science of outer space. Astronomers are people who study the universe—the solar system, the stars, the planets. They try to understand how large the universe is and how many years it has existed. Astronomers don't measure distance in outer space the way we measure distance on Earth. Have you ever heard someone say something is "astronomical"? If you want to say that something is really big, such as distances in space, you can use the word *astronomical.*

Our sun is a star. It is closer to Earth than any other star in the universe. The sun is about 93 million miles away. The next nearest star after the sun is about 24 trillion miles away! Light from the sun has to travel pretty far to reach Earth. Light travels quickly, though—about 186,282 miles per second. The speed of light is always the same.

Scientists use the term *light-years* to refer to how far light travels in an Earth year. Astronomers use light-years as a way to measure the huge distances in outer space.

To find how many actual miles a light-year is, first calculate the number of seconds in a year: 60 seconds × 60 minutes × 24 hours × 365.25 days in a year = 31,557,600 seconds. Then multiply the number of seconds in a year by the speed of light (186,282 miles per second). So, one light-year is about 5,878,612,843,200 miles. That means in one year, light can travel about 6 trillion miles through space. But this is still only about one-fourth the distance to the nearest star to our sun. When talking about the size of the universe, a single light-year is very small.

Many astronomers believe that the universe began with an explosive blast, known as the Big Bang. The Big Bang, they believe, created all the matter that would become planets and stars. Astronomers think the universe is now about 11.2 billion years old. Light that is reaching us from the farthest known galaxies has been traveling for more than 20 billion years.

A galaxy is a collection of billions of stars and clouds of gases and dust. The Milky Way is the name of our galaxy. It includes our sun, with its nine known planets, and billions of other stars. Look at the stars some night. Some of the light you see may have started out from stars billions of years ago.

Reading Time ______

Recalling Facts

1. Astronomers study
   - ❑ a. the Earth.
   - ❑ b. the influence of stars on people.
   - ❑ c. the solar system, the stars, and the planets.

2. A light-year is
   - ❑ a. an amount of time.
   - ❑ b. equal to 6 million miles.
   - ❑ c. a unit for measuring distance.

3. The speed of light is about
   - ❑ a. 186,000 miles per second.
   - ❑ b. 24 trillion miles per second.
   - ❑ c. 6 billion miles per second.

4. The Big Bang is believed to have
   - ❑ a. occurred 37 billion years ago.
   - ❑ b. destroyed millions of planets.
   - ❑ c. created the material that formed the universe.

5. The Milky Way is
   - ❑ a. a galaxy.
   - ❑ b. a solar system.
   - ❑ c. a planet.

Understanding Ideas

6. The light of the sun travels ______ to Mars as it does to Earth.
   - ❑ a. at a slower speed
   - ❑ b. at a faster speed
   - ❑ c. at the same speed

7. An astronomer would agree that a light-year
   - ❑ a. is easier to use than miles are for measuring distance in space.
   - ❑ b. is really smaller than a mile in space.
   - ❑ c. is used to measure the light of stars.

8. Light from the sun reaches Earth in less than one light-year because
   - ❑ a. the distance from the sun is measured in miles, not light-years.
   - ❑ b. the sun is less than 6 trillion miles away.
   - ❑ c. the sun is in the same galaxy as Earth.

9. The main idea of the Big Bang is that the universe was created when
   - ❑ a. materials exploded and then scattered.
   - ❑ b. materials formed from the blast and then scattered.
   - ❑ c. an explosive blast caused materials to scatter.

10. One can conclude from this passage that
    - ❑ a. the planets will someday be stars.
    - ❑ b. time travels more slowly in space.
    - ❑ c. light from some stars may have taken billions of years to reach Earth.

14 B Finding the Mean Distance from the Sun

There are nine known planets in our solar system. We generally think of them in order by their distance from the sun. All the planets orbit the sun in the same direction. Also, each is closer to the sun at some times than at other times. This is why scientists talk about a planet's mean distance from the sun. The mean is the average of two or more numbers. In the case of a planet's orbit, the mean is the average of the greatest distance and the shortest distance from the planet to the sun.

Earth's mean distance from the sun is 93 million miles. But astronomers do not like to use such big numbers when talking about the immense distances in space. That is why they measure these distances in smaller astronomical units. One astronomical unit, or 1AU, is Earth's mean distance from the sun. In other words, 1AU = 93 million miles.

When Earth is closest to the sun, the distance between the two is about 91.3 million miles. At the point in its orbit farthest from the sun, Earth is 94.5 million miles away. Scientists take an average of these numbers, $(91.3 + 94.5) \div 2$, and then round the quotient to 93 million miles.

1. Recognizing Words in Context

Find the word *immense* in the passage. One definition below is closest to the meaning of that word. One definition has the opposite or nearly the opposite meaning. The remaining definition has a completely different meaning. Label the definitions C for *closest,* O for *opposite or nearly opposite,* and D for *different.*

_______ a. wide

_______ b. tiny

_______ c. huge

2. Distinguishing Fact from Opinion

Two of the statements below present *facts,* which can be proved. The other statement is an *opinion,* which expresses someone's thoughts or beliefs. Label the statements F for *fact* and O for *opinion.*

_______ a. The mean distance between Earth and the sun is about 93 million miles.

_______ b. All planets orbit the sun in the same direction.

_______ c. Earth is the most important planet.

3. Keeping Events in Order

Number the items below 1, 2, and 3 to show the order in which the steps should be performed.

_____ a. Define one astronomical unit as 93 million miles.

_____ b. Find the smallest and largest distances between Earth and the sun.

_____ c. Find the average distance between Earth and the sun.

4. Making Correct Inferences

Two of the statements below are correct *inferences,* or reasonable guesses. They are based on information in the passage. The other statement is an incorrect, or faulty, inference. Label the statements C for *correct* inference and F for *faulty* inference.

_____ a. A planet with a smaller AU number than Earth's has a shorter mean distance from the sun.

_____ b. Planets are never the same distance from the sun at different points in their orbits because their orbits are not perfectly even.

_____ c. A tenth planet will never be found.

5. Understanding Main Ideas

One of the statements below expresses the main idea of the passage. One statement is too general, or too broad. The other explains only part of the passage; it is too narrow. Label the statements M for *main idea,* B for *too broad,* and N for *too narrow.*

_____ a. Astronomers use astronomical units to refer to how far each planet is from the sun.

_____ b. When determining astronomical units, the mean distance is the average of the greatest and shortest distances.

_____ c. Planets are closer to the sun at some times than at other times.

Correct Answers, Part A _____

Correct Answers, Part B _____

Total Correct Answers _____

15 A What Do Business Accountants Do?

Accountants gather and organize financial information for company owners. This information helps owners understand the finances of their company. In a way, an accountant records the history of a company in dollar amounts collected and paid out.

Business accountants list all the money a company has made or lost on a form called a general ledger. This form shows asset accounts and liability accounts. Assets may be money that is gained or materials that are worth money. Liability is money owed to some person or another company.

Some costs appear on both the assets side and the liabilities side of the ledger. Others show up on only one side. Buying a machine for $100 in cash would show up on only the assets side. The machine's value—$100—would be added to the company's equipment assets. The same amount would be subtracted from its cash assets. The net change in total assets would be zero. However, if the company bought the machine on credit, both sides of the ledger would be affected. The equipment assets would increase by $100, but the liabilities would also increase by $100.

An accountant records every change that involves money as both a debit item and a credit item. These debits and credits are called "entries" because they are entered into the general ledger. A credit entry may be money available to spend. A debit entry shows how money was spent. This system of accounting is known as double-entry accounting.

Keeping financial records is the most common task of accountants. However, many accountants work in specific areas. Some large companies hire accountants to design record-keeping computer programs for them. Many accountants work on creating better budgets for companies. Others may focus on ways to increase a company's profits. Tax accountants prepare tax returns. They may advise company presidents about how new business deals may affect taxes. Tax accountants must know a lot about laws that apply to taxes.

Some accountants work as auditors. These people study financial statements to make sure they are complete and correct. Auditors who work in a company make sure that the company's accounting plan is being followed. Outside auditors make sure a company's financial statements are correct and that the company follows the accepted accounting rules. Accountants have a lot of responsibility, so they must be well trained. They must pass a difficult test before they can get a license.

Reading Time ______

Recalling Facts

1. Any changes that involve money are recorded as
   - ❑ a. credits.
   - ❑ b. debits.
   - ❑ c. both credits and debits.

2. Liability is
   - ❑ a. money a company has made.
   - ❑ b. a credit.
   - ❑ c. money owed to a person or company.

3. A company's assets
   - ❑ a. may be materials that are worth money.
   - ❑ b. are its expenses.
   - ❑ c. always take the form of cash.

4. An auditor's job is to
   - ❑ a. design record-keeping computer programs for companies.
   - ❑ b. create better budgets for companies.
   - ❑ c. make sure financial statements are correct and complete.

5. Which of the following is *not* a true statement?
   - ❑ a. Every change that involves money is called a ledger because these changes are entered into the general ledger.
   - ❑ b. Accountants must have a license to work.
   - ❑ c. Tax accountants must know a lot about laws that apply to taxes.

Understanding Ideas

6. One can infer from this passage that
   - ❑ a. accounting is an important part of every business.
   - ❑ b. accounting is more important for large businesses than for small ones.
   - ❑ c. accountants generally have their own ways of keeping records.

7. If a company bought a cash register priced at $2,500 on credit,
   - ❑ a. its assets would decrease by $2,500.
   - ❑ b. both its assets and its liabilities would increase by $2,500.
   - ❑ c. its liabilities would decrease by $2,500.

8. One can infer from the passage that a tax accountant
   - ❑ a. decides whether a company pays taxes.
   - ❑ b. makes sure the company does not break any tax laws.
   - ❑ c. writes new tax laws for the company to follow.

9. Of the following, one job an accountant would *not* do is
   - ❑ a. suggest ways to save money.
   - ❑ b. buy new equipment.
   - ❑ c. keep track of how much the company pays its workers.

10. If a company is losing money, an accountant probably would first
    - ❑ a. think of new ways to cut company costs.
    - ❑ b. design a program for keeping better records.
    - ❑ c. look for the cause in the general ledger.

15 B Home Office Deductions

Working from a home office can have tax rewards. A person with a home office could deduct some of the costs of the home office from his or her taxes.

The Internal Revenue Service has rules about what counts as a home office. The worker must use the office for business only. Tax rules allow a worker to deduct a percentage of certain costs for the home according to the percentage of the house that is used as office space. Imagine that a person's house has 2,000 square feet. The office fills 200 square feet. To find the percentage of tax deduction, divide the total square feet of the house by the square feet of the office (2,000 ÷ 200 = 10). This means that 10 percent of the costs for the home can be deducted from the taxes.

The worker can also deduct 10 percent of the direct costs of the home office. For example, let's say that one year office machines ($11,000), heat and electricity ($3,590), and a new carpet ($1,720) for the home office came to $16,310. The worker would be allowed to subtract 10 percent of this amount, or $1,631, from the taxes.

1. Recognizing Words in Context

Find the word *deduct* in the passage. One definition below is closest to the meaning of that word. One definition has the opposite or nearly the opposite meaning. The remaining definition has a completely different meaning. Label the definitions C for *closest,* O for *opposite or nearly opposite,* and D for *different.*

_____ a. take away

_____ b. add

_____ c. set apart

2. Distinguishing Fact from Opinion

Two of the statements below present *facts,* which can be proved. The other statement is an *opinion,* which expresses someone's thoughts or beliefs. Label the statements F for *fact* and O for *opinion.*

_____ a. The Internal Revenue Service sets the rules for deductions for home offices.

_____ b. The Internal Revenue Service is too strict in its rules for home office deductions.

_____ c. Workers can deduct 10 percent of the direct costs of a home office space.

3. Keeping Events in Order

Number the steps below 1, 2, and 3 to show the order of the steps as described in the passage.

______ a. The worker deducts a percentage of the direct costs of the office space.

______ b. The worker decides to use the office for business only.

______ c. The worker determines the percentage of the house that is used as office space.

4. Making Correct Inferences

Two of the statements below are correct *inferences,* or reasonable guesses. They are based on information in the passage. The other statement is an incorrect, or faulty, inference. Label the statements C for *correct* inference and F for *faulty* inference.

______ a. Home office deductions help workers earn more.

______ b. If you sometimes use your home office for business reasons, you can claim a home office deduction.

______ c. Incorrect deductions taken for a home office could result in a fine by the Internal Revenue Service.

5. Understanding Main Ideas

One of the statements below expresses the main idea of the passage. One statement is too general, or too broad. The other explains only part of the passage; it is too narrow. Label the statements M for *main idea,* B for *too broad,* and N for *too narrow.*

______ a. The Internal Revenue Service has rules for home office deductions.

______ b. Home office deductions are popular with workers.

______ c. Home office deductions allow people who work at home to save money on their taxes.

Correct Answers, Part A ______

Correct Answers, Part B ______

Total Correct Answers ______

Answer Key

Reading Rate Graph

Comprehension Score Graph

Comprehension Skills Profile Graph

Answer Key

1A	1. c	2. a	3. b	4. c	5. b	6. c	7. b	8. c	9. a	10. b
1B	1. C, D, O	2. F, O, F	3. 3, 1, 2	4. C, C, F	5. B, M, N					
2A	1. b	2. c	3. b	4. c	5. c	6. a	7. a	8. a	9. b	10. a
2B	1. C, O, D	2. F, O, F	3. 2, 3, 1	4. F, C, C	5. N, M, B					
3A	1. b	2. c	3. b	4. b	5. a	6. c	7. a	8. c	9. a	10. c
3B	1. C, O, D	2. F, O, F	3. 2, 1, 3	4. C, C, F	5. M, B, N					
4A	1. a	2. a	3. b	4. a	5. b	6. a	7. c	8. a	9. c	10. a
4B	1. C, O, D	2. F, F, O	3. 1, 2, 3	4. C, F, C	5. M, N, B					
5A	1. c	2. a	3. c	4. a	5. a	6. b	7. a	8. c	9. b	10. a
5B	1. D, C, O	2. F, F, O	3. 2, 3, 1	4. C, F, C	5. B, N, M					
6A	1. a	2. c	3. b	4. c	5. c	6. b	7. c	8. a	9. c	10. a
6B	1. O, C, D	2. F, O, F	3. 2, 3, 1	4. C, C, F	5. B, N, M					
7A	1. b	2. a	3. b	4. a	5. b	6. a	7. a	8. c	9. a	10. c
7B	1. D, O, C	2. O, F, F	3. 3, 2, 1	4. F, C, C	5. M, N, B					
8A	1. c	2. b	3. c	4. b	5. c	6. b	7. a	8. c	9. a	10. c
8B	1. O, D, C	2. F, F, O	3. 3, 1, 2	4. C, F, C	5. N, M, B					

9A	1. c	2. b	3. a	4. a	5. b	6. a	7. c	8. c	9. a	10. c
9B	1. O, D, C	2. F, O, F	3. 2, 3, 1	4. C, F, C	5. B, N, M					
10A	1. b	2. a	3. c	4. c	5. a	6. c	7. a	8. a	9. b	10. a
10B	1. C, D, O	2. F, F, O	3. 3, 1, 2	4. C, F, C	5. B, N, M					
11A	1. c	2. a	3. c	4. c	5. c	6. b	7. a	8. c	9. b	10. b
11B	1. D, O, C	2. F, O, F	3. S, A, S	4. F, C, C	5. B, N, M					
12A	1. a	2. c	3. a	4. a	5. a	6. c	7. a	8. c	9. a	10. a
12B	1. C, O, D	2. F, O, F	3. 2, 3, 1	4. C, C, F	5. M, N, B					
13A	1. c	2. b	3. b	4. c	5. c	6. a	7. b	8. b	9. c	10. c
13B	1. D, O, C	2. F, F, O	3. 2, 1, 3	4. C, F, C	5. M, B, N					
14A	1. c	2. c	3. a	4. c	5. a	6. c	7. a	8. b	9. b	10. c
14B	1. D, O, C	2. F, F, O	3. 3, 1, 2	4. C, C, F	5. M, N, B					
15A	1. c	2. c	3. a	4. c	5. a	6. a	7. b	8. b	9. b	10. c
15B	1. C, O, D	2. F, O, F	3. 3, 1, 2	4. C, F, C	5. N, B, M					

Reading Rate

Put an X on the line above each lesson number to show your reading time and words-per-minute rate for that lesson.

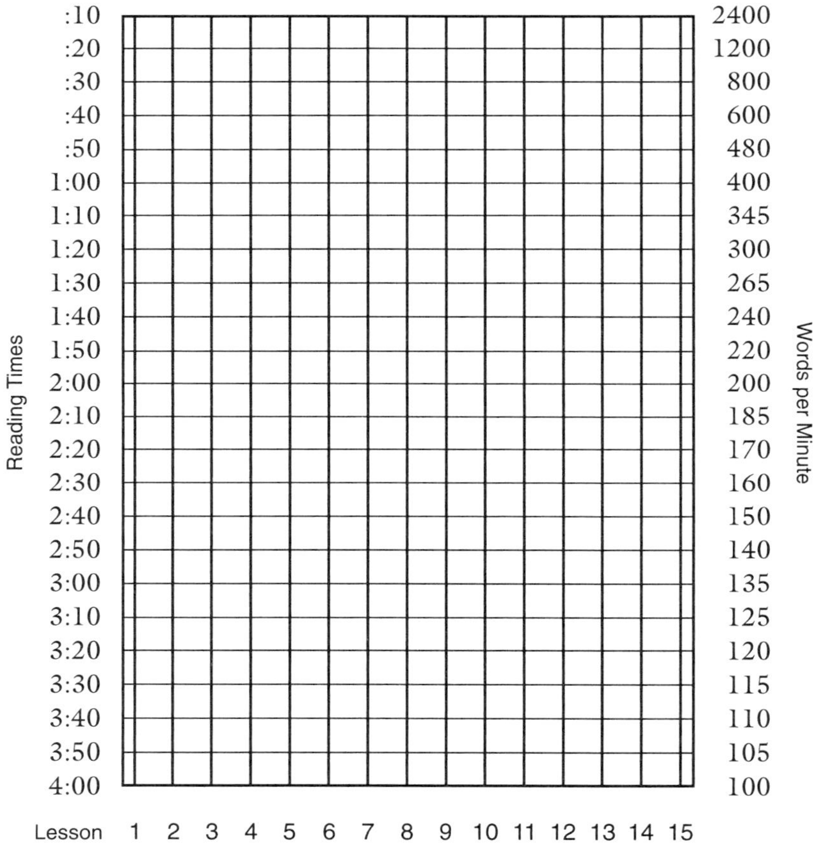

Comprehension Score

Put an X on the line above each lesson number to indicate your total correct answers and comprehension score for that lesson.

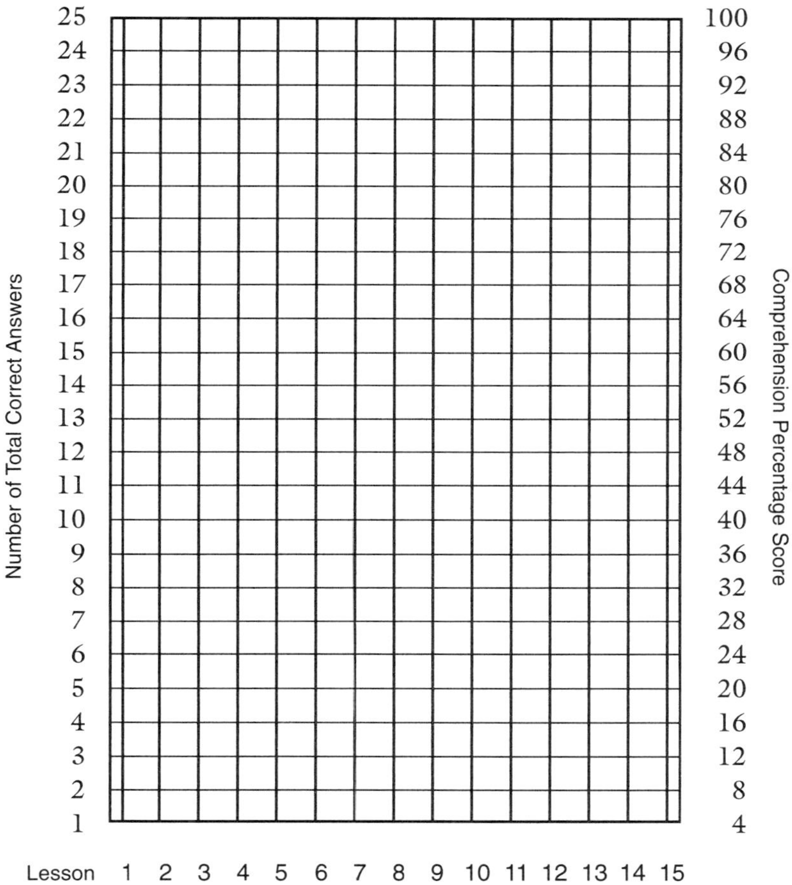

Comprehension Skills Profile

Put an X in the box above each question type to indicate an incorrect response to any part of that question.

Lesson	Recognizing Words in Context	Distinguishing Fact from Opinion	Keeping Events in Order	Making Correct Inferences	Understanding Main Ideas
Lesson 1					
2					
3					
4					
5					
6					
7					
8					
9					
10					
11					
12					
13					
14					
15					